Latin American Dictatorships in the Era of Fascism

Latin American Dictatorships in the Era of Fascism focuses on the reverse-wave of dictatorships that emerged in Latin America during the 1930s and the transnational dissemination of authoritarian institutions in the era of fascism.

António Costa Pinto revisits the study of authoritarian alternatives to liberal democracy in 1930s Latin America from the perspective of the diffusion of corporatism in the world of inter-war dictatorships. The book explores what drove the horizontal spread of corporatism in Latin America, the processes and direction of transnational diffusion, and how social and political corporatism became a central set of new institutions utilized by dictatorships during this era. These issues are studied through a transnational and comparative research design to reveal the extent of Latin America's participation during the corporatist wave which by 1942 had significantly reduced the number of democratic regimes in the world.

This book is essential reading for students studying Latin American history, 1930s dictatorships and authoritarianism, and the spread of corporatism.

António Costa Pinto is Research Professor at the Institute of Social Sciences, University of Lisbon. He has been a visiting professor at Stanford University, Georgetown University, and a senior visiting fellow at Princeton University, the University of California, Berkeley, and New York University. He is the author of *The Nature of Fascism Revisited* (2012) and co-edited *Rethinking Fascism and Dictatorship in Europe* (2014) and *Corporatism and Fascism* (2017).

Routledge Studies in Fascism and the Far Right
Series editors: Nigel Copsey, Teesside University, and Graham Macklin, Center for Research on Extremism (C-REX), University of Oslo

This new book series focuses upon fascist, far right and right-wing politics primarily within a historical context but also drawing on insights from other disciplinary perspectives. Its scope also includes radical-right populism, cultural manifestations of the far right and points of convergence and exchange with the mainstream and traditional right.

Titles include:

The March on Rome
Violence and the Rise of Italian Fascism
Giulia Albanese

Aurel Kolnai's 'War Against the West' Reconsidered
Edited by Wolfgang Bialas

The Ku Klux Klan and Freemasonry in 1920s America
Fighting Fraternities
Miguel Hernandez

The Lives and Afterlives of Enoch Powell
The Undying Political Animal
Edited by Olivier Esteves and Stéphane Porion

Latin American Dictatorships in the Era of Fascism
The Corporatist Wave
António Costa Pinto

For more information about this series, please visit: https://www.routledge.com/Routledge-Studies-in-Fascism-and-the-Far-Right/book-series/FFR

Latin American Dictatorships in the Era of Fascism
The Corporatist Wave

António Costa Pinto

LONDON AND NEW YORK

First published 2020
by Routledge
2 Park Square, Milton Park, Abingdon, Oxon OX14 4RN
and by Routledge
605 Third Avenue, New York, NY 10017
First issued in paperback 2021

Routledge is an imprint of the Taylor & Francis Group, an informa business

© 2020 António Costa Pinto

The right of António Costa Pinto to be identified as author of this work has been asserted by him in accordance with sections 77 and 78 of the Copyright, Designs and Patents Act 1988.

All rights reserved. No part of this book may be reprinted or reproduced or utilised in any form or by any electronic, mechanical, or other means, now known or hereafter invented, including photocopying and recording, or in any information storage or retrieval system, without permission in writing from the publishers.

Trademark notice: Product or corporate names may be trademarks or registered trademarks, and are used only for identification and explanation without intent to infringe.

British Library Cataloguing-in-Publication Data
A catalogue record for this book is available from the British Library

Library of Congress Cataloging-in-Publication Data
Names: Pinto, António Costa, author.
Title: Latin American dictatorships in the era of fascism: the corporatist wave / António Costa Pinto.
Description: London; New York, NY: Routledge/
Taylor & Francis Group, 2019.
Identifiers: LCCN 2019016626 | ISBN 9780367243852 (hardback) | ISBN 9780429282164 (ebk)
Subjects: LCSH: Latin America—Politics and government—20th century. | Latin America—History—20th century. | Dictatorship—Latin America—History—20th century. | Fascism—Latin America—History—20th century. | Authoritarianism—Latin America—History—20th century. | Corporate state—Latin America—History—20th century.
Classification: LCC F1414 .P58 2019 | DDC 980.03—dc23
LC record available at https://lccn.loc.gov/2019016626

ISBN 13: 978-0-367-78796-7 (pbk)
ISBN 13: 978-0-367-24385-2 (hbk)

Typeset in Times New Roman
by codeMantra

Contents

List of tables	vii
Preface	viii
Acknowledgements	ix
Introduction	1

PART I
Dictatorships and political institutions in the fascist era   5

1 Social and political corporatism during the first
   wave of democratization   7

2 The diffusion of corporatism in Latin America:
   the humus of social Catholicism, Action
   Française, and fascism   17

PART II
The worlds of dictatorships in Latin America   25

3 The 1930s authoritarian wave in Latin America   27

4 Uriburu and the failed corporatist dictatorship
   in Argentina   31

5 The dictatorship of Ibáñez and corporatism in Chile   41

6 Peru under Sánchez Cerro and Benavides   47

7 Rafael Franco and the 'Febrerista' regime in Paraguay	53
8 The Bolivia of David Toro: 'military socialism' with a fascist overtone	58
9 Gabriel Terra and the Uruguayan *Dictablanda*	62
10 The New State of Getúlio Vargas: the primacy of social corporatism in Brazil	68
11 Lázaro Cárdenas and the permutations of corporatism in authoritarian Mexico	85
12 Laureano Gómez and the failure of authoritarian corporatism in Colombia	98
13 The 'fascist era' in Latin America: the resilience of competitive authoritarianism: concluding remarks	108
Index	115

Tables

3.1	Authoritarian Regimes and their Leaders	28
11.1	The Four Sections of the *Partido de la Revolución Mexicana* (PRM)	88
13.1	Authoritarian Regimes, Parties, and Corporatism in Latin America	109

Preface

This book is an interpretive examination, from a transnational and comparative perspective, of Latin American dictatorships during the so-called fascist era. Its aim is to understand how and why the Latin American authoritarian regimes fit into the authoritarian wave of the 1930s and in the dynamic of the global spread of corporatist models during the inter-war period. This book is the result of a wider research project and is a kind of detour from the "Corporatism and Authoritarianism in Modern Politics" project that has already produced a number of publications in English and Portuguese.[1]

The first rule we give to young scholars when writing a book proposal or submitting an article for publication is that they should avoid the word 'gap'. As one anonymous reviewer once wrote about the author of a chapter in a book of mine: we do not write books or articles to fill gaps, after all, he wrote, 'we are not dentists. We do not fill gaps'. But quite frankly there was a gap to fill in this case, since there are few comparative studies of inter-war authoritarianism in Latin America. I hope this contribution will inspire more comparative and transnational research.

Note

1 A. C. Pinto and F. P. Martinho, eds., *A Onda Corporativa: Corporativismo e Ditaduras na Europa e na America Latina*, Rio de Janeiro, Editora da Fundação Getúlio Vargas, 2016, A. C. Pinto, ed., *Corporatism and Fascism: The Corporatist Wave in Europe*, London, Routledge, 2017; A. C. Pinto and F. Finchelstein, eds., *Authoritarianism and Corporatism in Europe and Latin America: Crossing Borders*, London, Routledge, 2019.

Acknowledgements

When I began writing this book, I remembered what Seymour Martin Lipset believed to be 'Linz's dilemma' (my own expression) when he noted this expert on authoritarianism and democratization adapted with difficulty to the academic outlets: writing too much for articles, and too little for books. In fact, the work produced by Juan Linz (1926–2013), a great political scientist whose work has been a big influence on me, was always halfway between articles and monographs. In my case, I had to severely cut my chapter, 'Authoritarianism and corporatism in Latin America: The first wave', in *Authoritarianism and Corporatism in Europe and Latin America*, which I co-edited with Federico Finchelstein and which gave rise to this volume. Nowadays, academic publications are much more flexible than they were in Linz's day.

This book began taking shape thank to the excellent bibliographic resources at the New York University library. There is a lot of Spanish and Portuguese language sources and bibliographies to consult, and my time there as a Remarque Fellow in 2017 was crucial to the development, as were the various short research missions in Brazil, particularly to the Getúlio Vargas Foundation in Rio de Janeiro, in Mexico City to take part in a seminar organized by Clara Lida and Ernesto Bohoslavsky at the Colégio de México, and to Buenos Aires at the invitation of Ernesto Bohoslavsky, to take part in a panel at CLACSO in 2018.

Parts of this research have been presented at some seminars and conferences. The first was the 'Crossing Borders: Intellectuals of the Right and Politics in Europe and Latin America – Transnational Perspectives' conference, and the second the 'Corporatism and "Organic" Representation between Authoritarianism and Democracy' workshop I co-organized at Lisbon University's Social Science Institute in November 2016 and January 2018 and in two seminars at the Getúlio Vargas Foundation School of Social Science in Rio de Janeiro, 26–27 June 2017, at the 'New Perspectives on Corporatism: Latin America and Iberian Corporatist Experiences' conference, and on 22–24 October 2018 at the NETCOR meeting, 'Authoritarianism, Corporatism and Democracy', both organized by Marco Vannuchi.

Parts of this book were also discussed in the panel 'Authoritarian Corporatism between Europe and Latin America' at the Lasa Meeting in Barcelona, co-organized with Pedro Ramos-Pinto, in May 2018; at the First Convention of the International Association for Comparative Fascist Studies (COMFAS), at the Central European University in Budapest in April 2018, thanks to Constantin Iordachi, and at the 'New Approaches to the Study of Dictatorships in Twentieth Century' conference at the S. Daniel Abraham Center for International and Regional Studies, Tel Aviv University, 14 May 2018, thanks to Rannaan Rein.

I would like to thank the following for their comments on earlier drafts and bibliographical information: Luciano Aronne de Abreu, Ernesto Boholavsky, Vera Cepeda, Victoria De Grazia, Paulo Drinot, Álvaro Garrido, Fabio Gentile, Annarita Gori, Ângela de Castro Gomes, Herbert Klein, Jorge lanzaro, Francisco Palomanes Martinho, Pedro Ramos-Pinto, Rannan Rein, Andrés Malamud, Antonio Muñoz Sánches, Melissa Teixeira, Marco Vannuchi, and Claudia Viscardi. I am particularly indebted to Federico Finchelstein and Aristotle Kallis, who read parts of the manuscript, to Kurk Weyland, for his very inspiring work, and to the two anonymous reviewers for the very useful comments.

As Seymour M. Lipset once said: 'A person who knows only one country basically knows no country well', but in comparative research with a strong empirical component and nine different national cases, mistakes (I hope small) are always present and the author welcomes comments and suggestions for further reading. When I met Philippe Schmitter for the first time and read his works on Portuguese and Brazilian corporatism, I did not think that I would come to revisit some of his research topics; however, I must point out that my experience as his student and his colleague has always been important.

Finally, and most importantly, I would like to make the final dedication to my two sons, Filipe Costa Pinto and Vicente Costa Pinto.

Introduction

In 1952, President Laureano Gómez tried (and failed) to reorganize political representation in Colombia along authoritarian corporatist lines, with this attempt perhaps being the end of the first wave of corporatism associated with the era of fascism. A Catholic corporatist with Francoist sympathies and authoritarian tendencies, and leader of the Colombian Conservative Party, Gómez hoped to bring about constitutional reform that would have transformed him into the president of a new authoritarian, paternalist, and more confessional state with an executive that was increasingly independent of the legislature and with a corporatist Senate.[1] This failed experiment marked the end of a time of authoritarian institutional reform inspired by corporatism, which was one of the most powerful authoritarian models of social and political representation to emerge during the first half of the twentieth century.[2]

This book revisits the study of authoritarian alternatives to liberal democracy in 1930s Latin America from the perspective of the diffusion of corporatism in the world of inter-war dictatorships and authoritarian elites. What drove the horizontal spread of corporatism in Latin America? What processes of transnational diffusion were set in motion and from where to where? How did social and political corporatism become a central set of new institutions created by dictatorships in the 1930s? At what type of critical junctures were they adopted? The book tackles these issues by adopting a transnational and comparative research design. We will operationalize the concepts of social and political corporatism and their particular application to the study of inter-war authoritarian regimes, and the carefully constructed balance between the theoretical-transnational and the case-study sections of the book will, we hope, contribute to the theoretical parameters of the study of both authoritarianism and corporatism. Our focus on political institutions associated with political and social corporatism captures a rich array of entanglements between authoritarian political actors, and we will also emphasize the impact of political learning and diffusion from seemingly successful institutional innovations and precedents elsewhere.[3] Powerful processes of institutional transfers were a hallmark of inter-war dictatorships, and we argue corporatism was at the forefront of this process of cross-national diffusion of authoritarian institutions in Latin America, both as a new form of organized interest co-optation by the state and of an authoritarian (and new) type of political representation that was an alternative to liberal democracy. To what extent and how Latin America participates in the corporatist wave is the subject of this book.

Transnational entanglements between dictatorships and corporatist ideologies generated a rich field of circulation of ideas and practices that shaped the experience of inter-war dictatorships far more than has previously been assumed.[4] With this book, we wish to move the research on inter-war dictatorships in Latin America to a relational and institutionalist perspective that scrutinizes processes of ideological, political, and institutional diffusion over the time and space of inter-war world.[5] In order to capture this dynamic process, the book has the following sequence.

In Chapter 1, I frame the concepts of social and political corporatism, defining the two faces of the relation between corporatism and dictatorship used in this book. During the 1930s, social corporatism became synonymous with the forced unification of organized interests into single units of employers and employees that were closely controlled by the state and which eliminated their independence: especially that of trade unions. Social corporatism offered autocrats a formalized system of interest representation to manage labour relations, legitimizing the repression of free labour unionism. However, during this period political corporatism was also (and in some cases mainly) used to refer to the comprehensive organization of political society beyond state-social groups relations seeking to replace liberal democracy with an anti-individualist system of representation. Much of the appeal of corporatism in the inter-war years was related with this doing 'away with the instability and conflict of representative democracy'.[6] It is from this perspective, we revisit the processes of the institutional crafting of social and political corporatism, exploring two axes: transnational diffusion of corporatism in Latin America, travelling models and debates and national experiences of institutionalization.

In Chapter 2, I deal with the main transnational agents of diffusion of corporatism in Latin America, giving particularly salience to the Catholic Church, and the main intellectual-politicians that introduced and developed corporatist proposals. The concept of the intellectual-politician will be used here to define those intellectuals who were participating in the institutional crafting of these regimes as formal or informal members of the decision-making elite (i.e. as advisers, deputies, cabinet members or party leaders). They provided space for interaction among politicians and the transnational intellectual arena, cementing ideological and political relations and models. As in Europe, and with the obvious exception of the paradigmatic case of Mexico under Cárdenas, the most important models were Italian Fascism, the Primo de Rivera dictatorship in Spain, and Salazar's New State in Portugal.

In the third part of the book, I analyse the institutionalization of Latin American authoritarian regimes during the 1930s and the introduction of corporatist institutions. Particular attention will be given to the 'critical junctures' of the consolidation (and failure of) of these regimes and the external models of institution building through a 'thick description' of nine Latin American regimes. The book as a whole, therefore, analyses corporatism as an ideology and, especially, as a practice of power that was widely shared, reformulated, and applied to Latin America during the so-called 'reverse' authoritarian wave of the inter-war period.[7]

Notes

1 J. D. Handerson, *Conservative Though in Twentieth Century Latin America: The Ideas of Laureano Gómez*, Athens, Center for Latin American Studies, 1988; D. Nicolás Motta, *Laureano Gómez Castro y su Proyeto de Reforma Constitucional (1951–73)*, Bogotá, Universidad de Rosario, 2008.
2 For the literature on Latin America, see the collection of articles of the 1970s of H. J. Wiarda, *Corporatism and National Development in Latin America*, Boulder, CO, Westview Press, 1981; J. M. Malloy, ed., *Authoritarianism and Corporatism in Latin America*, Pittsburgh, PA, University of Pittsburgh Press, 1976 (especially the chapter by Guillermo O'Donnell); R. B. Collier and D. Collier, *Shaping the Political Arena: Critical Junctures – the Labor Movement and Regime Dynamics in Latin America*, Princeton, NJ, Princeton University Press, 1991. For an anthology in Spanish, see J. Lanzaro, ed., *El Fin de Siglo del Corporativismo*, Caracas, Nueva Sociedad, 1998.
3 For a typology of outcomes of diffusion in this period, see K. Weyland, *Making Waves: Democratic Contention in Europe and Latin America since the Revolutions of 1848*, New York, NY, Cambridge University Press, 2014, pp. 35–77.
4 N. D. Musiedlak, ed., *Les Experiences Corporatives dans L'Aire Latine*, Bern, Peter Lang, 2010.

5 A. C. Pinto and A. Kallis, eds., *Rethinking Fascism and Dictatorship in Europe*, London, Palgrave, 2013.
6 J.-W. Muller, *Contesting Democracy: Political Ideas in Twentieth-Century Europe*, New Haven, CT, Yale University Press, 2011, p. 111.
7 S. P. Huntington, *The Third Wave: Democratization in the Late Twentieth Century*, Norman, University of Oklahoma Press, 1993, pp. 16–18.

Part I
Dictatorships and political institutions in the fascist era

1 Social and political corporatism during the first wave of democratization

When looking at twentieth-century dictatorships, we note some degree of institutional variation. Parties, cabinets, parliaments, corporatist assemblies, juntas, and a whole set of parallel and auxiliary structures of domination, mobilization, and control were symbols of the (often tense) diversity characterizing authoritarian regimes.[1] Some of these authoritarian institutions, created in the political laboratory of inter-war Europe, expanded across the globe, particularly the personalization of leadership, the single-party and organic-statist legislatures, and contemporaries of fascism realized some of these institutions could be durable. As the committed early-twentieth-century observer, Romanian academic, and politically authoritarian Mihail Manoilescu noted, 'of all the political and social creations of our century – which for the historian began in 1918 – there are two that have in a definitive way enriched humanity's patrimony ... corporatism and the single party'.[2] Manoilescu dedicated a study to each of these political institutions without knowing in 1936 that some aspects of the former would be long-lasting and that the latter would become one of the most durable political instruments of dictatorships.[3] In the world of inter-war dictatorships, however, both the single (and/or dominant) party and the corporatist bodies became the backbone for the institutionalization of these regimes.[4]

Corporatism put an indelible mark on the first decades of the twentieth century – during the inter-war period particularly – both as a set of institutions created by the forced integration of organized interests (mainly independent unions) into the state and as an organic-statist type of political representation, alternative to liberal democracy.[5] Variants of corporatism inspired conservative, radical-right, and fascist parties, not to mention the Roman Catholic Church, the 'third way' favoured by some sections of the technocratic elites, and even some proposals coming from the left of the political spectrum.[6] But it mainly inspired the institutional crafting of dictatorships, from Benito Mussolini's Italy through Primo de Rivera in Spain or the Uriburu dictatorship in Argentina and New State in Brazil. Some of these dictatorships, such as Mussolini's Italy, made corporatism a universal alternative to economic liberalism, the symbol of a 'fascist internationalism'.[7] In peripheral Portugal, Salazarism also made an aborted attempt to establish a League of Universal Corporatist Action (Liga de Ação Universal Corporativa) that was much closer to the Catholic 'third way' as a diplomatic means to export the Portuguese corporatist model – the most durable of all the corporatist dictatorships, surviving from 1933 to 1974.[8] In fact, variants of corporatist ideology spread to the global world of dictatorships in the 1930s.[9]

Corporatism as an ideology and as a form of organized interest representation was promoted strongly by the Roman Catholic Church, from the late-nineteenth through to the mid-twentieth century, as a third way of social and economic organization in opposition to both socialism and liberal capitalism.[10] Much of the model predates the Papal encyclical, *Rerum Novarum* (1891), and was due to the romanticizing of medieval Europe's feudal guilds by nineteenth-century conservatives who had become disenchanted with liberalism and fearful of socialism and democracy.[11] Indeed, corporatist ideas became increasingly the vogue among younger Catholics frustrated with 'parliamentary' political Catholicism. However, 'the church's explicit endorsement surely moved corporatism from seminar rooms to presidential palaces', especially after the publication of the encyclical *Quadragesimo Anno* (1931).[12] Pope Pius XI assumed that as a result of the Great Depression, liberal capitalism and its associated political system were in decline and that new forms of economic and social organization were now needed.[13] The powerful intellectual and political presence of corporatism in the political culture of Catholic elites in both Europe and Latin America paved the way for other more secular influences.

Corporatism became a powerful ideological and institutional device against liberal democracy during the first half of the twentieth century, but the neo-corporatist practices of some democracies during its second half – not to speak of the use of the word within the social sciences in the 1970s and 1980s – demand a definition of the phenomenon being studied, and for the sake of conceptual clarity, to disentangle social from political corporatism:[14]

Social corporatism 'can be defined as a system of interest representation in which the constituent units are organized into a limited number of singular, compulsory, non-competitive, hierarchically-ordered and functionally-differentiated categories, recognized or licenced (if not created) by the state and granted a deliberate representational monopoly within their respective categories in exchange for observing certain controls on their selection of leaders and articulation of demands and support'.[15]

Political corporatism can be defined as a system of political representation based on an 'organic-statist' view of society in which its organic units (families, local powers, professional associations, and interest organizations and institutions) replace the individual-centred electoral model of representation and parliamentary legitimacy, becoming the primary and/or complementary legislative or advisory body of the ruler's executive.[16]

A central ideal of corporatist thinkers was the organic nature of society in the political and economic sphere. This was based on a critique of what Ugo Spirito called the egotistical and individualist *homo economicus* of liberal capitalism, which was to be replaced by a *homo corporativus*, who would be motivated by the national interest and common values and objectives.[17]

During the inter-war period, corporatism permeated the main political families of the conservative and authoritarian political right: from the Catholic parties and social Catholicism to radical-right royalists and fascists, not to speak of Durkheimian solidarists and supporters of technocratic governments associated with state-led modernization policies.[18] Royalists, republicans, technocrats, fascists, and social Catholics shared 'a notable degree of common ground on views about democracy and representation' and on the project of a functional representation as an alternative to liberal democracy, namely as constituencies of legislative chambers or councils that were established in many authoritarian regimes during the twentieth century.[19] However, there were differences between the Catholic corporatist formulations of the late nineteenth century and the integral corporatist proposals of some fascist and radical-right-wing parties. When we look at fascist party programmes and segments of the radical-right, like the Action Française-inspired movements, the picture is even clearer, with many reinforcing 'integral corporatism' vis-à-vis the social corporatism of Catholicism.

Although cut from the same ideological cloth, social and political corporatism did not necessarily follow the same path during the twentieth century. The historical experience with corporatism has not been confined to dictatorships, and in liberal democracies 'implicit tendencies towards corporatist structures developed both before and concurrently with the emergence of fascism'.[20] In fact, occupational representation was not limited to the world of dictatorships, with several democracies discovering complements to the typical parliamentary representation.[21] Corporatist ideology was a particularly powerful influence in Ireland's 1937 Constitution, for example, while several other inter-war bicameral democracies introduced corporatist representation to their upper chambers.[22] France in the 1930s became one of the most important locations for the spread of the most significant variant of corporatist ideologies, witnessing 'a veritable explosion of corporatist theorizing as intellectuals and politicians grappled with the implications of economic depression, social division and escalating international tension'.[23] In addition to the neo-socialists and technocrats, many jurists and conservative and Catholic economists translated, interpreted, and promoted corporatist alternatives, with significant transnational impact.[24]

Many ideologists of social corporatism – particularly within Catholic circles – advocated a societal corporatism without the omnipresent state, but the praxis of corporatist patterns of representation was mainly the result of an imposition by authoritarian political elites on civil society.[25] In fact,

> whatever pluralist elements there were in corporatism (notably the stress on the autonomy of corporations), they were annihilated by a foundational commitment to a supreme common good, infusing with a sense of purpose and direction a complex pyramidal edifice that had the state at its apex.[26]

Under inter-war dictatorships, social corporatism became synonymous with the forced unification of organized interests into single units of employers and employees that were tightly controlled by the state and eliminated their independence: especially the independence of the trade unions. Social corporatism offered autocrats a formalized system of interest representation with which to manage labour relations: legitimizing the repression of free labour unions through the co-optation of some of its groups in state-controlled unions, often with compulsory membership. Last but not least, corporatist arrangements also sought to 'allow the state, labour and business to express their interests and arrive at outcomes that are, first and foremost, satisfactory to the regime'.[27]

Despite some intellectual-politicians associated with dictatorships legitimizing themselves with a *corporatisme d'association* that was closer to social Catholicism, or which had some modernizing projects, the model adopted by the great majority of dictatorships was much closer to fascist statism. As one French observer noted in 1942, after studying the practices of five dictatorships, '*corporatisme d'association* is seen as the only true corporatism [...] and it does not exist!'[28] In practical terms, the institutionalization of social corporatism in most dictatorships followed models close to the proclamations contained in the Italian Labour Charter (Carta del Lavoro), thereby demonstrating its primacy.[29] State intervention, a large imbalance between business and labour associations (with the former having greater influence and the independence of the latter eliminated) and the creation of strong para-state institutions, was typical of almost all the corporatist experiments. In fact, the elimination of free unions and their forced integration into the state was the dominant characteristic.

However, during this period corporatism was also used to refer to the comprehensive organization of political society beyond state-social groups relations seeking to replace liberal democracy with an anti-individualist system of representation.[30] As Williamson noted, 'what did unite the corporatist was their indifference to the concept of democracy and democratic norms' and from this it was just a small step to corporations as a representational structure.[31] Corporatist theorists presented a reasonable diversity of the 'organic basis of representation drawing on the permanent forces of society', in their alternatives to liberal democracy, but as the Marquis de La Tour du Pin (1834–1924) noted, this representation must be 'essentially consultative'.[32] The curtailment of this new legislature's powers and the autonomy of an executive with a head of government who is not responsible to parliament is an almost universal proposal of corporatists in early-twentieth-century politics.

George Valois, the syndicalist ideologist of Action Française and founder of one of the first French fascist movements, encapsulated the functions of corporatist legislatures when he proposed the replacement of parliament with general estates (*etats géneraux*).

> This body was not to be an assembly in which decisions were made based on majority votes or where the majority would be able to overwhelm the minority; rather, it was to be an assembly in which the corporations adjusted their interests in favour of the national interest.[33]

From this perspective, corporatism was an extremely appealing proposal for crafting and a powerful agent for the institutional hybridization of inter-war dictatorships, largely surpassing the ground from which it sprang.[34]

12 Dictatorships and political institutions

Since representation is an essential element of modern political systems, authoritarian regimes tended to create political institutions in which the function of corporatism was to give legitimation to organic representation and to ensure the co-optation and control of sections of the elite and organized interests.

> Working out policy concessions requires an institutional setting: some forum to which access can be controlled, where demands can be revealed without appearing as acts of resistance, where compromises can be hammered out without undue public scrutiny and where the resulting agreements can be dressed in a legalistic form and publicized as such.[35]

Another implicit goal of the adoption of corporatist representation, Max Weber noted, was to disenfranchise large sectors of society.[36] As Juan Linz states, 'corporatism encourages the basic apoliticism of the population and transforms issues into technical decisions and problems of administration'.[37]

Institutionalized, in many cases in the wake of polarized democratizations, inter-war dictatorships tended to choose corporatism both as a process for the repression and co-optation of the labour movement, interest groups, and of elites through 'organic' legislatures. Nevertheless, if the introduction of social corporatism was associated with the dictatorships of the first half of the twentieth century, their transformation into the base element of 'organic representation' in the new authoritarian political institutions, particularly the 'corporatist parliaments', was much more diverse, even if its spread was much more rapid. The constitutions, constitutional revisions, and their authoritarian equivalents are a clear indication of this dynamic.[38]

In many cases, the corporatist or economic parliaments either coexisted with and assisted parliaments or replaced them with a new legislature with consultative functions, which provided the government with technical assistance. The most influential theorist of *Quadragesimo Anno*, the Jesuit Heirich Pesch, did mention the economic parliament as a 'central clearing house' of his organic view, but he left its structure to the future.[39] With *Rerum Novarum*, the corporatism frame became clearer, with a corporatist reorganization of society associated with the strong anti-secular principals of parliamentary democracy held by Pope Pius XII.[40] In 1937, Karl Loewenstein saw 'this romantic concept of organic representation' in new legislatures trying to be a 'true mirror of the social forces of the nation and a genuine replica of its economic structure'.[41] However, the role of corporatist

Social and political corporatism 13

bodies within the dictatorships was, as we will see below, much less romantic. The curtailment of this new legislature's powers and the autonomy of an executive with a head of government who is not responsible to parliament is an almost universal proposal of corporatists in early-twentieth-century Europe and Latin America.

It is from this perspective we revisit in the next section, the transnational diffusion and main travelling models of corporatism in Latin America.

Notes

1 A. Perlmutter, *Modern Authoritarianism: A Comparative Institutional Analysis*, New Haven, CT, Yale University Press, 1981, p. 10.
2 M. Manoilescu, *Le Parti Unique: Institution Politique des Régimes Nouveaux*, Paris, Les Oeuvres Françaises, 1936, p. viii. On Manoilescu see C. Iordachi, 'Mihail Manoilescu and the debate and practice of corporatism in Romania', in Pinto and Finchelstein, eds., *Authoritarianism and Corporatism in Europe and Latin America*, pp. 65–94.
3 M. Manoilescu, *Le Siècle du Corporatisme*, Paris, Librairie Félix Alcan, 1934.
4 For a more developed version of this chapter, see A. C. Pinto, 'Corporatism and "organic representation" in European dictatorships', in Pinto, ed., *Corporatism and Fascism: The Corporatist Wave in Europe*, pp. 3–41.
5 Like Alfred Stepan and Juan Linz, we use this expression to refer to the 'vision of political community in which the component parts of society harmoniously combine ... and also because of the assumption that such harmony requires power and the unity of civil society by "the architectonic action of public authorities" – hence "organic-statism".' See A. Stepan, *The State and Society: Peru in Comparative Perspective*, Princeton, NJ, Princeton University Press, 1978; J. J. Linz, *Totalitarian and Authoritarian Regimes*, Boulder, CO, Lynne Rienner, 2000, pp. 215–17.
6 See P. J. Williamson, *Varieties of Corporatism: A Conceptual Discussion*, Cambridge, Cambridge University Press, 1985; C. S. Maier, *Recasting Bourgeois Europe: Stabilization in France, Germany, and Italy in the Decade after World War I*, Princeton, NJ, Princeton University Press, 1975 (2015).
7 On the expansion of corporatist 'internationalist thought' attempted in Fascist Italy, see S. Cassese, *Lo Stato Fascista*, Bologna, Il Mulino, 2010, pp. 89–98; J. Steffek, 'Fascist internationalism', *Millenium: Journal of International Studies*, Volume 44, 2015, pp. 3–22; M. Pasetti, *L'Europa Corporativa: Una Storia Transnazionale tra le due Guerre Mondiali*, Bologna, Bononia University Press, 2016.
8 Cardoso and Ferreira, "The corporatism chamber of the "New State" in Portugal: organized interests and public policy", Pinto, ed., *Corporatism and Fascism*, pp. 174–97; M. de Lucena, *A Evolução do Sistema Corporativo Português*, Vol. 1: *O Salazarismo*, Lisbon, Perspectivas e Realidades, 1976; H. J. Wiarda, *Corporatism and Development: The Portuguese Experience*, Amherst, University of Massachusetts Press, 1977; J. M. T. Castilho, *Os Procuradores à Camara Corporativa, 1935–1974*, Lisbon, Texto, 2010.

14 *Dictatorships and political institutions*

9 Musiedlak, ed., *Les Experiences Corporatives dans L'Aire Latine*; T. Parla and A. Davison, *Corporatist Ideology in Kemalist Turkey: Progress or Order?*, Syracuse, NY, Syracuse University Press, 2004; M. Franke, 'Fascist Italy: Ideal template for India's economic development?', in H. Schultz-Forberg, ed., *Zero Hours: Conceptual Insecurities and New Beginnings in the Interwar Period*, Brussels, P. I. E. Peter Lang, 2013, pp. 77–115; R. Hofmann, *The Fascist Effect: Japan and Italy, 1915–1952*, Ithaca, NY, Cornell University Press, 2015; M. Clinton, *Revolutionary Nativism: Fascism and Culture in China, 1925–1937*, Durham, NC, Duke University Press, 2017.

10 S. Solari, 'The corporative third way in social Catholicism (1830–1918)', *European Journal of History of Economic Thought*, Volume 17, Number 1, February 2010, pp. 87–113; P. Misner, *Catholic Labor Movements in Europe: Social Thought and Action, 1914–1965*, Washington, DC, The Catholic University of America Press, 2015.

11 See O. von Gierke, *Political Theories of the Middle Age*, London, Cambridge University Press, 1922.

12 R. Morck and B. Yeung, 'Corporatism and the ghost of the third way', *Capitalism and Society*, Volume 5, Number 3, 2010, p. 4.

13 See J. F. Pollard, *The Papacy in the Age of Totalitarianism, 1914–1958*, Oxford, Oxford University Press, 2014.

14 For an overview of this literature on corporatism, the 'new corporatism' and neo-corporatism, see P. J. Williamson, *Varieties of Corporatism: Corporatism in Perspective*, London, Sage, 1989.

15 P. C. Schmitter, 'Still the century of corporatism?', in F. B. Pike and T. Stritch, eds., *The New Corporatism: Social-Political Structures in the Iberian World*, Notre Dame, IN, Notre Dame University Press, 1974, p. 94. As Howard Wiarda noted, even when associated with different kinds of political regime, this definition 'was still tied to the more authoritarian versions [...]'. See H. J. Wiarda, 'The political sociology of a concept: Corporatism and the "distinct tradition"', *The Americas*, Volume 66, Number 1, July 2009, p. 90.

16 My definition, in A. C. Pinto, *The Nature of Fascism Revisited*, New York, NY, SSM-Columbia University Press, 2012, p. 122.

17 C. Bastien and J. L. Cardoso, 'From *homo economicus* to *homo corporativus*: A neglected critique of neo-classical economics', *The Journal of Social Economics*, Volume 36, 2007, pp. 118–27.

18 O. Dard, 'Le corporatisme entre traditionalistes et modenisateurs: Des groupements aux cercles du pouvoir', in Musiedlak, *Les experiences corporatives*, pp. 67–102. V. Torreggiani, *Stato e culture corporative nel Regno Unito: Progetti per una rappresentanza degli interessi economici nella riflessione inglese della prima metà del XX secolo*, Milan, Giuffré, 2018.

19 Williamson, *Corporatism in Perspective*, p. 32.

20 L. Panitch, 'The development of corporatism in liberal democracies', *Comparative Political Studies*, Volume 10, Number 1, 1977, p. 629.

21 See S. F. Riquelme, 'La era del corporativismo: La representación jurídica-política del trabajo en la Europa del siglo XX', *Revista de Estudios Histórico-Jurídicos*, Volume XXXI, 2009, pp. 399–425.

22 K. Loewenstein, 'Occupational representation and the idea of an economic parliament', *Social Science*, Volume 12, October 1937, p. 426. On Ireland

see as an element of the debate within Catholic circles, E. J. Coyne, 'The vocational structure of Ireland', *The Irish Monthly*, Volume 66, Number 780, June 1938, pp. 394–402.
23 M. Hawkins, 'Corporatism and third-way discourses in inter-war France', *Journal of Political Ideologies*, Volume 7, Number 3, 2002, p. 302.
24 O. Dard, 'Vichy France and corporatism', in Pinto, ed., *Corporatism and Fascism*, pp. 216–35; A. Chatriot, 'Un débat politique incertain: Le corporatisme dans la France des années 1930', *Les Études Sociales*, Number 157–8, 2013, pp. 231–44.
25 Stepan, *The State and Society*, p. 47.
26 C. Laborde, *Pluralist Thought and the State in Britain and France, 1900–1925*, London, Macmillan, 2000, p. 165.
27 W. Kim and J. Gandhi, 'Co-opting workers under dictatorship', *The Journal of Politics*, Volume 72, Number 3, 2010, p. 648.
28 L. Baudin, *Le Corporatisme: Italie, Portugal, Allemagne, Espagne, France*, Paris, Libraire Generale de Droit et de Jurisprudence, 1942, p. 141.
29 See M. Pasetti, 'The fascist labour charter and its transnational spread', in Pinto, ed., *Corporatism and Fascism*, pp. 143–158; A. C. Pinto, 'Authoritarianism and corporatism in Latin America: The first wave', in Pinto and Finchelstein, eds., *Authoritarianism and Corporatism in Europe and Latin America*, pp. 118–213.
30 D. A. Chalmers, 'Corporatism and comparative politics', in H. J. Wiarda, ed., *New Directions in Comparative Politics*, Boulder, CO, Westview, 1991, p. 63.
31 Williamson, *Varieties of Corporatism*, p. 63.
32 Cit. in Ibid. p. 69.
33 See A. Chatriot, 'Georges Valois, la representation professionelle et le syndicalisme', in O. Dard, ed., *Georges Valois: Intinéraire et Receptions*, Berne, Peter Lang, 2011, p. 65.
34 On this process of hybridization in inter-war dictatorships see Pinto and Kallis, eds., *Rethinking Fascism and Dictatorship in Europe*.
35 J. Gandhi and A. Przeworski, 'Authoritarian institutions and the survival of autocrats', *Comparative Political Studies*, Volume 40, Number 11, 2007, p. 1282.
36 M. Weber, *Economy and Society: An Outline of Interpretive Sociology*, Berkeley, CA, University of California Press, 1968, pp. 1, 298.
37 And 'those chambers are only components in their regimes [...] no legislature in an authoritarian regime has either the formal or de facto power to question the ultimate authority of a ruler or ruling group'. See J. J. Linz, 'Legislatures in organic-statist-authoritarian regimes: The case of Spain', in J. Smith and L. D. Musolf, eds., *Legislatures in Development: Dynamics of Change in New and Old States*, Durham, NC, Duke University Press, 1979, pp. 91, 95.
38 See C. Thornhill, 'The rise and fall of corporatist constitutionalism: A sociological thesis', in Pinto, ed., *Corporatism and Fascism: The Corporatist Wave in Europe*, pp. 78–100; P. Velez, *Das Constituições dos Regimes Nacionalistas do Entre-Guerras*, Lisbon, Imprensa de Ciências Sociais, 2017. For Latin America, see R. Gargarella, *Latin American Constitutionalism, 1810–2010: The Engine Room of the Constitution*, New York, NY, Oxford University Press, 2013, pp. 105–31.

39 P. Misner, 'Christian democratic social policy: Precedents for third-way thinking', in T. Kselman and J. A. Buttigieg, eds., *European Christian Democracy: Historical Legacies and Comparative Perspectives*, Notre Dame, IN, Notre Dame University Press, 2003, p. 77.
40 J. Backhaus, G. Chaloupek and H. Frambach, eds., *On the Economic Significance of the Catholic Social Doctrine: 125 Years of Rerum Novarum*, Cham, Springer, 2017.
41 K. Loewenstein, 'Occupational representation and the idea of an economic parliament', p. 423.

2 The diffusion of corporatism in Latin America
The humus of social Catholicism, Action Française, and fascism

In 1941, a *New York Times* journalist visited ten Latin American countries and wrote an article expressing his concerns about Catholic sympathies towards corporatism, dictatorships, and even 'totalitarian' fascism, across the continent. After many conversations with bishops, priests, and lay Catholic leaders, some of whom were critics of the US, he concluded: 'Repeatedly one heard from priests and laymen throughout South America the view that the Salazar dictatorship in Portugal was an almost ideal state, and this seemed to be accepted as a fairly general Catholic view'.[1] More thorough research could have added more European references, namely the Primo de Rivera dictatorship in Spain and Italian Fascism, but the predominant association between Catholicism and authoritarianism was obviously captured well by this American journalist.

Social Catholicism pre-empted the spread of corporatism in Latin America. The Roman Catholic Church and its associated lay organizations, and intellectuals, following the publication of the Papal encyclicals *Rerum Novarum* (1891) and especially *Quadragesimo Anno* (1931), became central transnational agents in the introduction of corporatist alternatives to the excesses of liberal capitalism. As in other parts of the world in the first half of the twentieth century, the official Church looked for ways to regain its role in society, and the proliferation of lay Catholic organizations was crucial for the spread of corporatism.[2] Organized and directed by Catholic clergymen, associations such as Catholic Action sought to enhance the involvement of Catholics in social and political structures. Part of the Church's response to secularism, socialism, and Protestantism, in the words of Pope Pius X in 1903, it sought to bring about the 're-Christianization' of society.[3] During the 1930s, the official Church and its thinkers made corporatism an alternative to communism and liberal democracy, and 'the task of the era was to forge a modern Catholicism that could make its peace with the new authoritarianism'.[4] A 1936 letter from French Cardinals, celebrating 'corporation, with its cadres, its hierarchy, its regulatory power, its jurisdiction and its right of representation in government', was without doubt repeated in various forms across Europe and Latin America.[5]

In Argentina during the 1930s, such influential figures as Monsignor Gustavo Franceschi articulated a type of reactionary 'national Catholicism' that was based on a 'home-grown right-wing ideological posture that equated Argentine national identity with Catholicism'.[6] In Brazil, convergence between the authoritarian corporatism of the Church and politics was also clear, even with some convergence with the fascists of Plínio Salgado's Brazilian Integralist Action (AIB – Ação Integralista Brasileira).[7] In particular, Cardinal Sebastião Leme, archbishop of Rio de Janeiro from 1930 to 1942, viewed Getúlio Vargas and his corporatist Estado Novo (New State) as being 'consistent with the Church's hierarchical vision of society'.[8] It is important to remember, though, that the Church and state conciliation did not proceed without conflict or that there were versions of social Catholicism that were more compatible with liberal democracy. In Chile, the split between the young Catholics, Manuel Antonio Garretón with his *hispanismo* and corporatism and Eduardo Frei, future leader the Christian Democratic Party, is just one example.[9]

It is in this context that Catholic intellectuals, in many cases priests and friars, crossed the Atlantic Ocean and Latin American borders several times. The Catholic press gave voice to an impressive process that spread social and political corporatist ideas throughout Latin America. Among the names mentioned on both sides of the Atlantic were those of two Spanish Jesuits, Father Palau and Joaquín Azpiazu, who were ardent defenders of Catholic corporatism.[10] The Jesuits were important in the spread of corporatist ideas in Latin America, so much so that other names could be mentioned: men such as Restrepo in Colombia and Miguel Bullrich and Luis Chagnon in Argentina. Azpiazu, whose writings constantly appeared in the Catholic press, was probably the most important.[11] The more moderate Félix Restrepo did not eliminate democracy from his corporatism, which was curiously associated with Oliveira Salazar's New State in Portugal. For Restrepo 'corporatism re-establishes the lost equilibrium, realizing the project of the Creator in the world of labour'.[12] Azpiazu, however, claimed corporatism was the basis of the 'totalitarian state': 'Strong [...] without the weakness and hesitations of the liberal and socialist state'.[13]

Of course, the Catholic Church was not alone in fanning the flames of corporatism in Latin America.[14] The influence of new European traditionalist radical-right thinking was also very important, and this was not in conflict, since the Catholic milieu 'was the main recipient of Maurassianism' after the First World War, in a strict association with the 'Catholic revival'.[15] In Argentina, for example, the synchronicity was clear from the 1920s in such magazines as *Criterio* and the writings of Monsignor Franceschi.[16] In Brazil, the magazine *A Ordem* and Jackson de Figueiredo's Dom Vital Centre promoted the same Catholic restoration programme, and called for the 'regeneration of the nation', which it claimed was being threatened by mass 'immigration, Judaism and communism'.[17] Again, 'the movement of men from both sides of the Atlantic is the decisive factor in the spread of Maurasianism in Latin America'.[18] When we examine the corpus of the new authoritarian nationalist constructs in Brazil, Argentina, Chile, Peru, and many other Latin American countries, we see a very impressive influence of Action Française, blended with the corresponding Iberian elite movements – Acción Española in Spain and Integralismo Lusitano in Portugal.[19] Many Latin American intellectual-politicians who collaborated closely with the dictators who were associated with the institutionalization of corporatism in Latin America came from this cultural background: from José de la Riva-Agüero in Peru to Leopoldo Lugones and the Irazusta brothers in Argentina.

The Spanish intellectual Ramiro de Maeztu (1875–1936), one of the most influential in Latin America, is probably the clearest example of these transatlantic cultural transfers.[20] The principal ideologue of the Primo de Rivera dictatorship and a critic of liberal democracy, who unified *hispanismo* and corporatism, Maeztu was a towering intellectual presence in Latin America.[21] An ambassador to Argentina of Primo de Rivera in the late 1920s, he was even more important because of the union between traditionalist Catholicism with Action Française-inspired intellectuals in the Iberian-Latin American conservative milieus during the first half of the twentieth century, to which was added active anti-US views.[22]

The domestic fascist parties were another tool for diffusion of integral corporatist ideas that often completed and radicalized the local social Catholic culture.[23] Dozens of fascist parties emerged in Latin America during the 1930s, many of which were no larger than small political groups with little impact.[24] Most were modelled on Italian Fascism, although some were closer to German National Socialism. Earlier immigration to Latin America from Spain, Italy, and Germany ensured the extremist political culture of these countries was present in the Latin American political arenas. Nevertheless, as in Europe, even those closest culturally to German National Socialism were closer programmatically to Italian Fascism and there, despite their diversity and different abilities to mobilize, corporatism was contained in all their political manifestos. This was true in Brazil and Peru, where fascist movements had the greatest political and electoral success, where the AIB of Plínio Salgado and the Revolutionary Union (UR – Unión Revolucionaria) of Luis A. Flores presented political corporatism as their political banner, not to mention the clerico-fascism of the Mexican synarchists.[25] In the case of the AIB, the integral state it called for in its manifestos was an organic whole, and its national secretary for doctrine, Miguel Reale, stressed integral corporatism would be the New State's representation model.[26] The 'totalitarian corporatist state' was also the political goal of the UR in Peru.[27] In all their diversity, the smaller and more mimetic Latin American fascist parties faced the same direction, with them all eventually copying the Italian model more directly; however, their influence was limited.

As elsewhere in the world, including Europe, many of these fascist parties were not recognized as such by Italian officials, with the reports to Rome being very pessimistic and critical except in the case of the more important parties, such as the AIB.[28] The strategy employed by Italian diplomats and Fascist institutions met with more success among conservative political and intellectual elites, including the Catholic clergy and sections of the armed forces.

The economic crisis of 1929 paved the way for a 'true Fascist Italy geopolitics in Latin America', particularly towards new authoritarian regimes, including the Uriburu dictatorship in Argentina, that of Busch in Bolivia, Vargas in Brazil, Benavides in Peru, and Terra in Uruguay.[29] With the export of Fascist corporatism, Italy also sought to develop a cultural model of Pan-Latinism, although with less success.[30]

When looking at the European authoritarian models, those most mentioned in 1930s Latin America are the Portuguese New State, Italian Fascism, and the Primo de Rivera dictatorship in Spain, with the Italian Labour Charter and corporatist representation as the two main features.[31] To varying degrees, the ideological background described above shared these references whenever events brought them close to power.

Franco Savarino provided a good summary of what these regimes had to offer authoritarian leaders in 1930s Latin America (although he was referring to Italian Fascism):

> a modernizing policy (nationalist, corporatist, mobilizing) capable of strengthening national communities, consolidating states, enhancing authoritarian leadership and proposing changes to the geopolitical balance that are more favourable both to the emerging

powers and the dependent 'peripheries' [...] From this perspective, it can be said Fascism sought a pragmatic and utilitarian way of solving specific problems and to find a way forward.[32]

By the late 1930s, US diplomacy started to express concerns about the 'fascist influence' in Latin America. As the American journalist quoted at the start of this section noted, these models do not 'coincide with the traditional American view of the desirable state' and represent 'a considerable obstacle to Pan-American understanding and, consequently, to collective defence'.[33] In Latin America thought, the New Deal response to the crisis of 1929 was challenging the corporatists answers, and by the mid-1930s it had become 'an international trade mark [...] and a source of inspiration as well', with interventionist options that were more friendly to democracy.[34]

In the next section, we describe Latin American participation in the authoritarian wave of the 1930s, with its impressive cohort of authoritarian regimes that were more diverse in nature and less institutionalized than their European counterparts.

Notes

1 H. Callender, 'Latin Catholics suspicious of US South America churchmen not entirely sympathetic to democratic Ideas', *New York Times*, 3 August 1941.
2 L. M. Edwards, 'Messages sent, messages received? The papacy and the Latin American church at the turn of the twentieth century', in S. J. C. Andes and J. C. Young, eds., *Local Church, Global Church: Catholic Activism in Latin America from Rerum Novarum to Vatican II*, Washington, DC, Catholic University of America Press, 2016, pp. 3–20.
3 B. L. Hernández Sandoval, 'The revival of Latin American Catholicism, 1900–60', in V. Garrard-Burnett, P. Freston and S. C. Dove, eds., *The Cambridge History of Religions in Latin America*, Cambridge, Cambridge University Press, 2016, pp. 346–58.
4 J. Chappel, *Catholic Modern: The Challenge of Totalitarianism and the Remaking of the Church*, Cambridge, MA, Harvard University Press, 2018, p. 63.
5 Cit. in Chappel, Ibid., p. 87.
6 Sandoval, 'The revival', p. 355.
7 L. P. Gonçalves, *Plínio Salgado: Um Católico Integralista entre o Brasil e Portugal*, Lisbon, Imprensa de Ciências Sociais, 2017.
8 Sandoval, 'The revival', p. 352.
9 S. Correa, 'El corporativismo com expresión politica del social cristianismo', *Teologia y Vida*, Volume XLIX, 2008, pp. 467–81; Y. Contreras-Vejar, 'Unorthodox fate: The rise of Chile's Christian Democratic Party', *Journal of Religious and Political Practice*, Volume 1, Number 1, 2015, pp. 58–72.
10 J. Azpiazu, *El estado corporativo*, Madrid, Razón y Fe, 1934.

22 Dictatorships and political institutions

11 See S. Fernández Riquelme, 'Joaquín Azpiazu y la Sociología cristiana: Nota biografica e intelectual', *La Razón Histórica*, Volume 6, 2009, pp. 42–49.
12 F. Restrepo, *Corporativismo*, Bogota, Revista Javeriana, 1939, p. 32.
13 J. Azpiazu, *El Estado Católico: Líneas de un Ideal*, Madrid, Rayfe, 1937, p. 29.
14 For the case of Ecuador, see C. R. E. Fernández de Córdova, 'Repensar la derecha: Democracia cristiana, corporativismo e integralismo en Ecuador en la entreguerra (1918–1943)', *Historia*, Volume 396, Number 2, 2018, pp. 55–90.
15 O. Compagnon, 'Le maurrassisme en Amérique Latine: Étude comparée des cas argentin et brésilien', in O. Dard and M. Grunewald, eds., *Charles Maurras et l'étranger – L'étranger et Charles Maurras*, Berne, Peter Lang, 2009, p. 287.
16 Compagnon, 'Le maurrassisme', p. 287.
17 See J. J. V. de Sousa, *Círculos Operários: A Igreja Católica e o Mundo do Trabalho no Brasil*, Rio de Janeiro, Editora da UFRJ, 2002; C. M. Rodrigues, *A Ordem: Uma Revista de Intelectuais Católicos, 1934–1945*, São Paulo, Autêntica, 2005.
18 Compagnon, 'Le maurrassisme', p. 296.
19 A. C. Pinto, *The Blue Shirts: Portuguese Fascism in Interwar Europe*, New York, NY, SSM-Columbia University Press, 2000.
20 See P. C. González Cuevas, *Maeztu: Biografía de un Nacionalista Español*, Madrid, Marcial Pons Historia, 2003 and V. Torreggiani, 'A travelling intellectual of a travelling theory: Ramiro de Maeztu as a transnational agent of corporatism', in Pinto and Finchelstein, eds., *Authoritarianism and Corporatism in Europe and Latin America*, pp. 159–79.
21 For more on *hispanismo* and the relationship between reactionary intellectuals and Iberian-Latin American conservatives, see F. B. Pike, *Hispanismo, 1898–1936: Spanish Conservatives and Liberals and their Relations with Spanish America*, Notre Dame, IN, University of Notre Dame Press, 1971.
22 On his influence in Chile, see J. Díaz Nieva, *Chile: De la Falange Nacional a la Democracia Cristiana*, Madrid, Universidad Nacional de Educación a Distancia, 2000.
23 See S. McGee Deutsch, *Las Derechas: The Extreme Right in Argentina, Brazil, and Chile, 1890–1939*, Stanford, CA, Stanford University Press, 1999.
24 See S. U. Larsen, ed., *Fascism Outside Europe: The European Impulse Against Domestic Conditions in the Diffusion of Global Fascism*, New York, NY, SSM-Columbia University Press, 2001; H. Trindade, *O Nazi-Fascismo na América Latina: Mito e Realidade*, Porto Alegre, UFRGS, 2004; F. Savarino, 'Fascismo en America Latina: La perspectiva italiana (1922–1943)', *Diálogos*, Volume 14, Number 1, 2010, pp. 39–81.
25 See H. Trindade, *Integralismo: O Fascismo Brasileiro na Década de 30*, São Paulo, Difel, 1974; J. F. Bertonha, *Integralismo: Problemas, Perspectivas e Questões Historiográficas*, Maringá, Editora da Universidade Estadual de Maringá, 2014; J. Meyer, *El Sinarquismo, el Cardenismo y la Iglesia (1937–1947)*, Mexico City, Tusquets, 2003.
26 M. Reale, *O Estado Moderno*, Rio de Janeiro, José Olympio, 1934.

27 T. A. Molinari Morales, *El Fascismo en el Perú: La Unión Revolucionaria, 1931–1936*, Lima, Universidad Nacional Mayor de S. Marcos, 2006.
28 See J. F. Bertonha, *Fascismo e Antifascismo Italianos: Ensaios*, Caxias do Sul, Editora da Universidade de Caxias do Sul, 2017, pp. 47–69.
29 F. Savarino, 'Italia y América Latina: Política, diplomacia y geopolítica, 1920–1950', *Enfoque Social*, Volume 2, 2007, p. 30.
30 C. Brandalise, 'O conceito de América Latina: Hispano-americanos e a panlatinidade europeia', *Cuadernos del CILHA*, Volume 18, 2013, pp. 1–31.
31 See M. Pasetti, 'From Rome to Latin America: The transatlantic influence of Fascist corporatism', in Pinto and Finchelstein, eds., *Authoritarian and Corporatism in Europe and Latin America*, pp. 143–158.
32 F. Savarino, 'Juego de ilusiones: Brasil, México y los "fascismos" latinoamericanos frente al fascismo italiano', *Historia Crítica*, Volume 37, 2009, p. 136.
33 Callender, 'Latin Catholics'.
34 K. K. Patel, *The New Deal: A Global History*, Princeton, NJ, Princeton University Press, 2016, p. 239.

Part II
The worlds of dictatorships in Latin America

3 The 1930s authoritarian wave in Latin America

Latin America participated in what has been called the first wave of democratization, and in the subsequent reverse wave that by 1942 had significantly reduced the number of democratic regimes in the world.[1] Regardless of the political regime classification adopted or the different periodization, by the early 1930s – and especially during the Great Depression – there was 'a surge of reactionary regimes (that) reduced the proportion of competitive systems to a low of 19 per cent in 1943'.[2] Between 1930 and 1934, there were thirteen successful coups, followed by a further seven in the last years of the decade.[3] During this time, an impressive spectrum of authoritarian regimes was established, some of which were very instable and poorly institutionalized, while others were more consolidated.

The year 1930 was a pivotal year 'in Latin American history due to the number of regime changes that took place'.[4] In Argentina, President Hipólito Yrigoyen was removed from power by a military coup led by General José Félix Uriburu, which was typical of the events of that decade. 'A democratic government overthrown by military intervention backed by the conservative classes, who attempted to create a system of limited participation, which preferably did not depend on elections, adopting some version of the corporatist institutions established in Italy'.[5] In Brazil that October, General Tasso Fragoso prevented an elected president from taking office, although the consequent appointment of Getúlio Vargas did not lead to an immediate break with liberalism – that did not happen until 1937 with the establishment of the Estado Novo (New State). In Peru in 1930, President Augusto Leguía was overthrown by Colonel Luis Miguel Sánchez Cerro. In Uruguay, President Gabriel Terra established a dictatorship in 1933. In 1936 in Bolivia and Paraguay, coups by Colonel David Toro and Rafael Franco, respectively, paved the way for authoritarian regimes. Across much of Central America, the old oligarchical politics also lost ground

Table 3.1 Authoritarian Regimes and their Leaders

Country	Regime	Period
Argentina	Uriburu	1930–32
Bolívia	David Toro	1936–37
	Germán Busch	1937–39
Brazil	Getúlio Vargas	1937–45
Chile	Ibañéz del Campo	1927–31
	Carlos Dávila Espinoza	1932
Colombia	Laureano Goméz	1950–53
México	Lázaro Cárdenas	1934–40
Paraguay	Rafael Franco	1936–37
	Félix Estegarrabia	1937–40
Peru	Sánchez Cerro	1931–33
	Oscar Benavides	1933–39
Uruguay	Gabriel Terra	1933–38
	Alfredo Baldomir	1938–42

to authoritarian strongmen. By 1939, few Latin American countries remained liberal democracies (Table 3.1).[6]

The 1929 crisis worsened some elements of crises of liberal democratic regimes, although with different impacts. As in Europe, it was not easy to find in Latin America the determining factor for the rise of authoritarianism with the Great Depression. There is in fact a wider range of variation, with it proving difficult to discern 'common political patterns riding on the back of the common economic experience of the Depression'.[7] In Chile, for instance, the overthrow of General Carlos Ibáñez's dictatorship was pushed along due to the 1929 crises, while in Venezuela, Juan Vicente Gómez, a traditional dictator whose regime adopted some superficial 'social' traits in the early 1930s, had been in power since 1909. Nevertheless, even if 'there was no strict rule regarding Depression-induced political change', there was a clear move towards economic dirigisme that 'tended to produce a conservative and authoritarian direction of travel'.[8] This process of state intervention in the economy and within interest groups increased the appeal of corporatist structures during the 1930s which were sometimes legitimized through the authoritarian experiences. Nevertheless, if social corporatism suppressed and dismantled independent labour organizations, using them as instruments of state policy, the same did not happened in Chile or Colombia under López Pumarejo. In the latter case, the legitimation of state intervention in the economy was clearly inspired by the New Deal, showing that 'democracy and capitalism could be reconciled despite the challenges of the Great Depression'.[9]

The nature of authoritarian regimes was also diverse, in terms of chronology and type, ranging from the *dictablanda* of Gabriel Terra in Uruguay to the authoritarian New State of Getúlio Vargas in Brazil, or the short-lived Dictatorship of Uriburu in Argentina to the durable, albeit instable, 'competitive authoritarianism' of Sánchez Cerro and Óscar Benavides in Peru or of Cárdenas in Mexico. The Mexico of Lázaro Cárdenas was perhaps the most singular example because it was very different in nature from the corporatist experiences in the southern part of the continent.

The authoritarian wave associated with corporatism also marked the authoritarian regimes of Central America. Nicaragua, General Maximiliano Hernández Martínez's San Salvador, and Fulgencio Batista's Cuba were also part of this cycle.[10] In Nicaragua, for example, authoritarian corporatism was a strong presence, and its ideological and political roots were very close to the Iberian and Catholic models, even here in direct 'response to the 'democratizing' effects of the US occupation'.[11] In Batista's Cuba, which rejected political corporatism in the 1940 Constitution, its presence was equally important.[12]

As has been noted several times, from both a comparative and transnational perspective, the authoritarian 'reverse wave' of the inter-war period was a process that was 'contaminated by mutual emulations that are affirmed in their national development (but which are) part of the same historical cycle'.[13] In the next section, we analyse the successes and failures of the processes of institutional reform in selected authoritarian regimes in 1930s Latin America in more detail, paying particular attention to how domestic political actors rely on the 'heuristics of availability' in order to pursue similar authoritarian changes while looking at institutional models of corporatism for their own countries.[14]

The 'thick description' presented below has a common structure that seeks to analyse the institutionalization of these regimes around the three axes that marked the majority of their contemporary dictatorships: the attempt to create single or dominant parties, the institutionalization of social and political corporatism, and the dominant models of the intellectual-politicians who took part in them.

Notes

1 Huntington, *The Third Wave: Democratization*, pp. 16–18.
2 S. Mainwaring and A. Pérez-Liñán, *Democracies and Dictatorships in Latin America: Emergence, Survival, and Fall*, New York, NY, Cambridge University Press, 2013, p. 72.

30 Dictatorships in Latin America

3 Numbers from P. Drake, *Between Tyranny and Anarchy: A History of Democracy in Latin America, 1800–2006*, Stanford, CA, Stanford University Press, 2009, p. 165.
4 T. Di Tella, *History of Political Parties in Twentieth-Century Latin America*, New Brunswick, NJ, Transaction, 2004, p. 43.
5 Di Tella, *History of Political Parties*, p. 43. For a brief introduction to these regimes, see especially Chapter 3, 'The military and corporatist onslaught: From the thirties to the Second World War'.
6 See P. H. Lewis, *Authoritarian Regimes in Latin America: Dictators, Despots, and Tyrants*, Lanham, MD, Rowman & Littlefield, 2006.
7 A. Knight, 'The Great Depression in Latin America: An overview', in A. Knight and P. Drinot, eds., *The Great Depression in Latin America*, Durham, NC, Duke University Press, 2014.
8 Knight, 'The Great Depression', p. 292.
9 Patel, *The New Deal*, p. 4.
10 On San Salvador see E. Ching, *Authoritarian El Salvador: Politics and the origins of the Military Regimes, 1880–1940*, Notre Dame, IN, University of Notre Dame Press, 2014.
11 M. Gobat, *Confronting the American Dream: Nicaragua under US Imperial Rule*, Durham, NC, Duke University Press, 2005, p. 231 (see especially chapter 8, 'Militarization via democratization: The US attack on caudillismo and the rise of authoritarian corporatism').
12 See R. Whitney, *State and Revolution in Cuba: Mass Mobilization and Political Change, 1920–1940*, Chapel Hill, NC, University of North Carolina Press, 2001; B. M. Carbonell, 'Cuban corporatism: Batista's three-year plan and a nation betrayed', in M. A. Font and A. Tinajero, eds., *Handbook on Cuban History, Literature and the Arts: New Perspectives on Historical and Contemporary Social Change*, London, Routledge, 2014, pp. 274–85; J. C. Guanche, 'La constitución de 1940: Una reinterpretación', *Cuban Studies*, Volume 45, Number 1, 2017, 66–88.
13 F. Gallego, 'La posguerra del Chaco en Bolivia: Excombatientes, "socialismo militar" y nacionalización de masas en un periodo de transición', *Revista Universitaria de Historia Militar*, Volume 7, Number 4, 2015, p. 27.
14 K. Weyland, 'Toward a new theory of institutional change', *World Politics*, Volume 60, Number 2, 2008, p. 291.

4 Uriburu and the failed corporatist dictatorship in Argentina

General Uriburu's 1930 coup, which overthrew the constitutional government of Hipólito Yrigoyen, was the first successful military intervention against democracy in Argentina.[1] The transition from oligarchic liberalism to democracy began with the publication of the Sáenz Peña Law in 1912, which established the secret ballot and obligatory male suffrage. During the 1920s, the Congress was increasingly dominated by the Radical Civic Union (UCR – Unión Cívica Radical), which also won the presidential elections of 1916, 1922, and 1928, eroding the electoral strength of the conservative parties.[2] This growing semi-loyal conservative opposition, and the impact of the 1929 crisis, was one of the factors behind the coup.[3]

Although supported by conservative civilian sectors, the coup was military, and while Uriburu was perhaps one of the people behind the programme to establish a more clearly authoritarian regime, this was not the case with the other generals, such as Agustín Pedro Justo, whose aims were vaguer, but included ending the domination of the UCR. Uriburu had some ideas about the regime to be put in place, and almost all of those in his inner circle had similar ideas. One of these, *personalista*, Juan P. Ramos, who the general had commissioned to study the political reforms to be implemented after the coup, had no doubt that he 'wanted to suppress political professionalism and change the parliamentary regime'. That system change was 'functional democracy' – 'The general had a profound knowledge of the latest European literature on corporatist representation' and this had made him aware of the Labour Charter.[4] The coup proclamation was written by Leopoldo Lugones, a renowned nationalist intellectual and fascist admirer, and later moderated by one of Uriburu's assistants.[5] Uriburu's manifesto, which was published some weeks after the coup, both stated officially that it intended to 'create a new national grouping that would proclaim and sustain other ideas' and that 'when the representatives of the people cease to be merely representatives of political committees and occupy the congressional seats of workers, ranchers, farmers, professionals, industrialists, etc, democracy will be more than just a beautiful word among us'.[6]

Other intellectual-politicians close to Uriburu had no doubts about his programme to institutionalize corporatist representation, legitimated in the anti-party proposals of his 'functional democracy'.[7] A second, albeit restrained, aspect present during the early speeches was the idea that a 'new national force' must be created in the event of elections and constitutional reform. In the many conversations he had before the coup, Uriburu was much more explicit about his aims: to reform the Constitution, replace Congress with corporatist institutions, change the party system, and abolish the Sáenz Peña law.[8] As he stated bluntly to a small group of conspirators before the coup, 'I'm not an enemy of parliament, but I believe it must be organized other way. It seems to me that corporatist representation is the most practical'.[9]

For some students of Uriburu's dictatorship, his main inspiration – the Primo de Rivera regime in Spain – illustrates the 'interconnection of the two transatlantic coasts' in his presentation of himself as an authoritarian regenerator and moraliser of Argentine public life.[10] With more or less inspiration, however, the corporatist reform and the project of creation of a government-led dominant party incorporated Uriburu into the 'spirit of the age'.[11]

While the regime party did not see the light of day, Uriburu quickly established a paramilitary organization. Some months after the coup the Argentine Civic Legion (LCA – Legión Cívica Argentina) was created, modelled on Primo de Rivera's Somatén Nacional. While in theory the LCA was an independent organization, in May 1931 it became an 'official' militia, which soon began repressing opposition movements, as it did in April 1931 following the Radicals' unexpected victory over the conservatives in elections to the provincial Governor of the Buenos Aires.[12] Uriburu saw in the development of this militia a new political player with a role in the 'institutional reconstruction that the country demands based on the [corporatist] reforms we presented', but LCA was still an embryonic political organization when he left the presidency.[13]

The role of several intellectual-politicians associated with the radical-right in Uriburu's authoritarian and corporatist programmatic outlines was so evident that it deserves further comment. While few had had formal political roles, some – including Leopoldo Lugones, Carlos Ibarguren (Uriburu's cousin), Juan Carulla, and the Irazusta brothers – had been part of Uriburu's circle since the late 1920s, and were the authors of several political and constitutional reform proposals during his brief dictatorship. Their cultural and political influence was to be decisive in the fascist and authoritarian alternatives proposed in Argentina during the 1930s.[14]

The Catholic Church was another exponent of openly reactionary traditionalism that believed corporatism was the authoritarian solution for Argentina. Authoritarian Catholic intellectuals and activists, like Father Gustavo Franceschi, articulated a corporatist social Catholicism that closely followed the models of European fascist and authoritarian regimes and of the Hispanidad movement of the early twentieth century, that was at the roots of a 'home-grown right-wing ideological stance that equated Argentine national identity with Catholicism'.[15] Father Julio Meinvielle was another exponent of this openly reactionary Catholic traditionalism. Although with some variation, this theologian was behind the education of many activists and members of the elite who attended Catholic culture courses, with corporatism 'becoming the central and consistent element of Catholic nationalism throughout the 1930s'.[16]

Some Catholic traditionalists converged in the nationalist movement, which was the main proponent of fascist and authoritarian corporatism in late 1920s Argentina.[17] 'Nationalism combined the anti-Semitism of the Nazis, the "proletarian" and aestheticized violence of Italian Fascism and the ultra-Catholic militarism of Spanish fascism'.[18] The nationalists did not create a party as much as an elitist movement present in a number of leagues by the end of the 1920s, from where they opposed the UCR governments led by President Yrigoyen.

The nationalists were the main creators of an authoritarian Argentinian national identity: one that was corporatist, Catholic, Hispanic, and which placed great stock on such values as hierarchy, anti-liberalism, and anti-communism, all with elements of xenophobia and anti-Semitism.[19] Some of these intellectuals, such as Leopoldo Lugones, were much closer to Italian Fascism, but the majority – including Meinvielle – sought synthesis between fascism and traditionalist Catholicism, which was also the position of the Irazusta brothers.[20] Most of their writings cited the Action Française of Charles Maurras and Acción Española: this was particularly true for the more notorious and influential corporatists in Latin America, such as the Spaniards Ramiro de Maeztu and Joaquín Azpiazu.[21] Its press was also noted for its support for corporatist experiences in Fascist Italy and in António de Oliveira Salazar's New State in Portugal.[22] The fascist economists, Gino Arias or Azpiazu, were regular contributors in its publications.[23]

The corporatist projects of the Argentinian nationalists (and some of the liberal conservatives) were obviously significantly different, with one more social and the other more political.[24] Leopoldo Lugones, who like some of his companions had been a socialist, was perhaps the most famous nationalist intellectual-politician to design a project for a corporatist state that had the military as its leaders and main institutional organizers. In books such as *La Grande Argentina* (*Great Argentina*) and *Política Revolucionaria* (*Revolutionary Politics*), he called for an executive of military men supported by a Congress of delegates from the corporations, which would function as first degree electoral colleges that would legislating on the executive power's proposals while being represented in the government.[25] The government would continue to be republican and representative, but of the 'effective totality of the nation', and not of the political parties.

Uriburu was a retired general whose first government was not a military junta and most of his ministers were conservative civilians as the new 'provincial interventors' who replaced Yrigoyen radicals.[26] His aides and advisers were closer to the nationalists, while some, including Carlos Ibarguren, who was Interventor for the Córdoba province, occupied more important political positions. During the first month of his presidency, the repression of the union movement and the radicals was heavy, but hesitations and divergences over the future reform of political system soon made themselves felt.

The liberal-conservative universe represented by General Justo and by the Interior Minister Sánchez Sorondo, forced Uriburu to be more moderate, but he reaffirmed several times his corporatist project, in public and in private.[27] Justo and many other conservatives had been 'associated with a longer national tradition, and preferred a return to the old days of conservative preponderance, if necessary with the help of some ballot box juggling, but without destroying the liberal institutions'.[28] In a meeting in October 1930, for example, Carlos Ibarguren's proposals for a new parliament in which popular opinion would be represented, while also granting representation to the established unions and corporations, was criticized by the National Democratic Federation (FND – Federación Nacional Democrática), around which the political parties that had initially supported the provisional government coalesced.[29]

Replying to criticism from liberal-conservative supporters of the regime who were accusing Uriburu of attempting to create a 'fascist parliament' he reaffirmed his support for a moderate version of corporatist representation that would complement liberal representation.[30]

Even so, the reaction against these proposals was strong and was criticized by the FND. A project to organize a municipal government in Buenos Aires, with which Rodolfo Irazusta had been entrusted, was dismissed by the president – apparently because of its corporatist nature.[31] Uriburu's shrinking margin for manoeuvre limited his options to just two: moderate corporatism or a return to constitutional legality.[32]

The nationalists were soon disillusioned and in March 1931 they presented a project for integral corporatism that almost broke with Uriburu. The constitutional projects elaborated by Julio Irazusta, Leopoldo Lugones, and others focused on a system of corporatist representation in two chambers: the Chamber of Representatives, which included unions and business organizations and the Senate, which included the archbishops, five generals, and two admirals, who would approve the laws and elect the President.[33] Carulla published a book in which he criticized the 'myth of the Constitution' and downplayed the chance of any further conciliation with liberalism.[34] In fact, the proposals for Uriburu's constitutional reform had a short and troubled life, even the moderate version of Ibarguren, and the nationalists experienced defeat at the hands of the 'professional politicians'.[35]

Uriburu's hesitations and fears of the power of the parties had been confirmed. With support from Justo, the reforms, which imposed changes to Article 37, which had sought to establish corporatist representation were rejected by the parties of the FDN, that continued to make pressure to the return of 'institutional normality'.[36] In June 1931, a government manifesto made it known that the reforms agreed with the parties had ruled out corporatist representation.[37] As Ibarguren noted with remarkable accuracy, 'The revolution lacked an organized civil force that was determined to act, and which would impel it forward as its leader had hoped'.[38] Uriburu's short reign thus ended with the return of institutional order and the election of General Justo to the presidency on 8 November 1931 – a position he took up in February 1932.

In Uriburu's resignation message, he stated that despite 'considering copying any foreign corporatist law to be a mistake' he continued to have a high opinion of the 'organization of professions and unions and the modification of the current party political structures so the social interests could have authentic and direct representation'.[39] In the meanwhile, President Justo reneged on his promise to introduce reforms to Congress. Creating a political alliance that enabled him to govern within the Constitution and with universal suffrage, although through what was known as 'the patriotic fraud', Justo heralded the beginning of what the nationalists and radicals called 'infamous decade' of conservative rule.[40]

The spirit of Uriburismo was maintained by the nationalist throughout the 1930s, and the 'would-be corporatist revolution' did not disappear altogether.[41] Several leagues based on the 'Uriburu myth' emerged during the 'infamous decade', although as Federico Finchelstein noted, they failed in their principal aim, which was to 'unify nationalism politically and lead it to victory'.[42] In fact, the proliferation of nationalist groups during the 1930s did not prevent them from pushing their project to reform the republic in the direction of corporatism through their influence in the armed forces. The Argentine Nationalist Alliance (ANA – Alianza Nacionalista Argentina), a breakaway from the LCA, led by a nephew of Uriburu who had close links with the military, was one such example, although divisions were the rule. Proposals for corporatism were also frequent suggestions within Catholic circles, even although the penetration of social Catholicism and of nationalism in the labour movement and social corporatist institutions introduced by the state were limited.[43] The dominant trend among the nationalists seems to have been finding appropriate models in Benito Mussolini's Italy, Salazar's Portugal, and, with the outbreak of the Spanish civil war, Francisco Franco's 'Nationalist' Spain.[44] As Ibarguren noted, the whole world appeared to be on the move towards a 'functional democracy' that had been institutionalized in many countries, but not in Argentina during the 'infamous decade'.[45] The nationalists, however, remained influential ideologically both through their connections with the Catholic Church and within sections of the armed forces, which helps explain 'the influence nationalism acquired in the military government that on 4 June 1943 overthrew the 'fraudulent republic'.[46] Nevertheless, while its ideals survived the 1930s, General Uriburu's dictatorship was short-lived, 'the rest were intellectual frenzies outside government, which required them to win power in order to see them realized'.[47]

In the mid-1930s, Justo and other members of the conservative elite openly defended anti-liberal projects, and in 1937 the president shifted to a more clearly authoritarianism in his speeches, which called for the creation of an 'organic, structured, technical democracy'.[48] In 1936 communists were outlawed, while in the Senate and other institutions, conservative politicians like Sánchez Sorondo openly legitimized their proposals to restrict political freedom and left-wing activism by advocating fascism and reactionary political Catholicism. Nonetheless, despite this polarization and the growing presence of fascism and anti-democratic movements, 'the country did not slip into an alternative political system', illustrating 'the resilience of republican liberal structures'.[49] The same could be said of state intervention in the economy and the 'New Deal' models, with a limited creation of social corporatism structures.[50] The failure of corporatism under Uriburu's leadership, which was the first experience of authoritarianism in Argentina, demonstrates that this was, simultaneously, the main tool for the consolidation of authoritarianism and for the resistance of the political parties (and parts of the military) that was decisive in its overthrow.

Some scholars suggest the 'organized community' under General Juan Perón's regime in Argentina, as 'the most philosophically complete example of fascist corporatism in Latin America', was the victory of Uriburu's corporatist options.[51] For others, 'the new president relied on the trade unions and employers; he flirted with a state unionism that was compatible with the party system over which he dominated, but not with corporatism'. That is to say, 'the triumph of Peronism thus contributed to corporatism's final defeat'.[52] Either way, Perón's 'justicialism' was noted for its social – not political – corporatism, despite there being no lack of opportunities.[53]

Notes

1 See F. Finchelstein, 'Corporatism, dictatorship and populism in Argentina', in Pinto and Finchelstein, eds., *Authoritarianism and Corporatism in Europe and Latin America*, pp. 237–53.
2 See J. Horowitz, *Argentina's Radical Party and Popular Mobilization, 1916–1930*, University Park, PA, Penn State University Press, 2008; E. Bohoslavsky, 'De la ilusión con la promesa democrática a la decepción con la democracia realmente existente: Los conservadores de Argentina (1916–1930)', in E. Bohoslavsky, D. Jorge and C. E. Lida, eds., *Las Derechas Ibero-Americanas entre la Gran Guerra y la Gran Depresión,* Mexico City, El Colegio de México, 2019.
3 E. Alemán and S. Saiegh, 'Political realignment and democratic breakdown in Argentina, 1916–1930', *Party Politics*, Volume 20, Number 6, 2014, pp. 849–63.
4 Cit. in G. Frontera, 'La reforma constitucional como objetivo de la Revolución de 1930', *Revista de Historia del Derecho*, Volume 23, 1995, p. 99.
5 A. Spektorowski, 'The making of an Argentine fascist: Leopoldo Lugones – From revolutionary left to radical nationalism', *History of Political Thought*, Volume 17, Number 1, 1996, pp. 79–108.
6 Cit. in Frontera, 'La reforma constitucional', p. 100.
7 C. Ibarguren, *La Historia que he Vivido*, Buenos Aires, Peuser, 1955.
8 J. Fernando Segovia, 'La revolución de 1930: Entre el corporativismo y la partidocracia", *Revista de Historia Americana y Argentina*, Volume 41, 2006, p. 9.
9 Cit. in F. Devoto, *Nacionalismo, Fascismo y Tradicionalismo en la Argentina Moderna: Una Historia*, Buenos Aires, Siglo XXI, 2002, p. 247.

10 M. Ángel Perfecto, 'La derecha radical en Argentina y España: Relaciones culturales e interdependencias', *Studia histórica: Historia Contemporánea*, Volume 33, 2015, p. 131.
11 In March 1931, he asked the Spanish intellectual Navarro Monzó to write a report on corporatism, synthesizing a conversation with him. See Devoto, *Nacionalismo, Fascismo y Tradicionalismo*, p. 271.
12 E. González Calleja, 'El Hispanismo autoritario español y el movimiento nacionalista argentino', *Hispania: Revista Española de Historia*, Volume 226, 2007, pp. 17–18.
13 J. F. Uriburu, *La Palabra del General Uriburu: Discursos, Manifiestos, Declaraciones y Cartas Publicadas durante su Gobierno*, Buenos Aires, Roldán, 2nd ed., 1933, p. 91.
14 F. Finchelstein, *Transatlantic Fascism: Ideology, Violence and the Sacred in Argentina, 1919–1945*, Durham, NC, Duke University Press, 2010, pp. 62–8.
15 Hernández Sandoval, 'The revival of Latin American Catholicism, 1900–1960', p. 352. See also Deutch, *Las Derechas*, pp. 240–4.
16 J. María Ghio, *La Iglesia Católica en la Política Argentina*, Buenos Aires, Prometeo, 2007, p. 85.
17 There is a large bibliography in English on Argentinian nationalism and its main ideologues. See D. Rock, *Authoritarian Argentina: The Nationalist Movement, Its History, and Its Impact*, Berkeley, CA, University of California Press, 1995; Deutsch, *Las Derechas*; A. Spektorowski, *The Origins of Argentina's Revolution of the Right*, Notre Dame, IN, University of Notre Dame Press, 2003.
18 Finchelstein, 'Corporatism, dictatorship and populism in Argentina', p. 240.
19 For more on anti-Semitism and the nationalists, see D. Lvovich, *Nacionalismo y Antisemitismo en la Argentina*, Buenos Aires, Ediciones B, 2003.
20 See Devoto, *Nacionalismo, Fascismo y Tradicionalismo*; O. Inés Echeverría, *Las Voces del Miedo: Los Intelectuales Autoritarios Argentinos en las Primeras Décadas del Siglo XX*, Rosario, Prohistoria, 2009.
21 Calleja, 'El Hispanismo autoritario', pp. 599–642; D. P. Papanikas, *La Iglesia de la Raza: La Iglesia Católica Española y la Construcción de la Identidad Nacional en Argentina, 1910–1930*, doctoral thesis in contemporary history, Universidad Autónoma de Madrid, 2012.
22 The model of Salazar's corporatism in Portugal was cited in *Critério*. See A. Ivereigh, *Catholicism and Politics in Argentina, 1810–1960*, London, Macmillan, 1995, p. 117.
23 J. Fernando Segovia, 'El modelo corporativista de estado en la Argentina, 1930–1945: Entre el derecho, la política y la ideología', *Revista de Historia del Derecho*, Volume 34, 2006, p. 301.
24 See C. Bukovac, *Las Ideas y Proyectos Corporativistas en la Argentina del Siglo XX*, Rosario, Universidad Nacional de Rosario, 2016.
25 L. Lugones, *La Grande Argentina*, Buenos Aires, Editorial Babel, 1930; *Política Revolucionaria*, Buenos Aires, Anaconda, 1931. See O. Echevería, 'Leopoldo Lugones, el estado equitativo y la sociedad militarizada: Una representación del autoritarismo argentino después del golpe de estado de 1930', *Anuario de Estudios Americanos*, Volume 6, Number 1, 2004, pp. 201–32.

Uriburu and failed corporatist dictatorship 39

26 R. A. Potash, *The Army and Politics in Argentina, 1928–1945*, Stanford, CA, Stanford University Press, 1969, p. 56.
27 In a conversation with Federico Pineda, for example, from the Independent Socialist Party, Uriburu 'maintained that an immense superior system would be the one that would base political power on grouping citizens in categories – trade unions, professional bodies, and corporations, divided according to interests. Only thus was it possible to escape domination by the committees of political parties', cit. in J. Luis Romero, *A History of Argentine Political Thought*, Stanford, CA, Stanford University Press, 1963, p. 232.
28 Di Tella, *History of Political Parties*, p. 44. On the fate of economic and political liberalism in this period, see J. A. Nállim, *Transformations and Crisis of Liberalism in Argentina, 1930–1955*, Pittsburgh, PA, University of Pittsburg Press, 2012.
29 Cit. in J. P. Gardinetti, 'El golpe de estado de 1930 y las ideas corporativistas', *Anales*, Volume 41, Facultad de Ciencias Jurídicas y Sociales, UNLP, 2011, p. 385.
30 Frontera, 'La reforma constitucional', p. 106.
31 Segovia, 'El modelo corporativista', p. 293.
32 Devoto, *Nacionalismo, Fascismo y Tradicionalismo*, pp. 252–7.
33 Perfecto, 'La derecha radical', p. 130; Segovia, 'La revolución de 1930', pp. 29–32.
34 J. Carulla, *Valor Ético de la Revolución del 6 de Setiembre de 1930*, Buenos Aires, Belgrano, 1931.
35 Frontera, 'La reforma constitucional como objetivo de la revolución del 30', pp. 95–154.
36 Ibid., p. 109.
37 Ibid., p. 111.
38 Ibarguren, *La Historia que he Vivido*, p. 431.
39 Ibid., p. 438.
40 Perfecto, 'La derecha radical', p. 133.
41 Spektorowski, *The Origins of Argentina's Revolution*, pp. 86–7; F. Finchelstein, *The Ideological Origins of the Dirty War: Fascism, Populism and Dictatorship in Twentieth Century Argentina*, New York, NY, Oxford University Press, 2014, pp. 33–51.
42 F. Finchelstein, *Fascismo, Liturgia e Imaginario: El Mito del General Uriburu y la Argentina Nacionalista*, Buenos Aires, Fondo de Cultura Económica, 2002, p. 27.
43 M. Rubinzal, 'Del elitismo al nacionalismo obrerista: La derecha argentina y la cuestión obrera en los años 30', *Entrepasados*, Volume 30, 2006, pp. 67–85; and, especially, 'El nacionalismo frente a la cuestión social en Argentina (1930–1943): Discursos, representaciones y prácticas de las derechas sobre el mundo del trabajo', doctoral thesis, Universidad Nacional de la Plata, 2012. See also R. P. Korzeniewicz, 'Labor Unrest in Argentina, 1930–1943', *Latin American Research Review*, Volume 28, Number 1, 1993, pp. 7–40.
44 L. Zanatta, *Dallo Stato Liberale alla Nazione Cattolica: Chiesa ed Esercito nelle Origini del Peronismo, 1930–1943*, Milan, FrancoAngeli, 1996.
45 Cit. in Segovia, 'El modelo corporativista', p. 27.
46 M. Inés Tato, 'Una reflexión acerca de la cultura política de la derecha en la Argentina de entreguerras', *Projeto História*, Volume 47, 2013, p. 179.

47 Segovia, 'El modelo corporatista', p. 385.
48 Cit. in Nállim, *Transformations and Crises of Liberalism*, p. 49.
49 Ibid., p. 66.
50 On debates on economic liberalism in the 1930s, see Nállim, Ibid., pp. 86–104.
51 Lewis, *Authoritarian Regimes*, p. 131. See also Finchelstein, *The Ideological Origins of the Dirty War*, p. 65–92.
52 Segovia, 'El modelo corporatista', p. 354.
53 Curiously, corporatist representation would be introduced in the new Chaco province that was created in 1951. According to the new provincial constitution, which was of short duration, half the members of the House of Representatives would be elected by popular vote, with the other half being "elected by citizens belonging to the professional bodies governed by the national law of professional associations of which the candidates must be members", cit. in H. Gambini, *Historia del Peronismo*, Vol. II, Buenos Aires, Editorial Planeta, 2001, p. 187.

5 The dictatorship of Ibáñez and corporatism in Chile

Chile's first 'flirtation with state corporatism' occurred during the military-based dictatorship of Carlos Ibáñez del Campo (1927–31).[1] While the crisis of 1929 did not reinforce his semi-authoritarian regime, it was one of the factors that brought his presidency to an end in 1931.[2] Corporatism played an important role in the political culture of Chilean elites, especially Catholic elites, segments of the conservative parties, and local versions of fascism, although it became less important during the second half of the 1930s.[3]

The 1924 military intervention put an end to the liberal-parliamentary regime in Chile, and in 1925 Colonel Ibañéz del Campo assumed the position of Minister of War in the governments of Arturo Alessandri and his successor Emiliano Figueroa, who would eventually become Minister of the Interior in 1927. In that same year, he took control of the country's government as Vice-President of the republic, from where he was elected President – a position he held until July 1931, when he was forced to resign in the context of social unrest associated with the 1929 crisis. Nevertheless, during the difficult year of 1932, after he left the country, Chile continued to be led by Ibañistas, such as Carlos Dávila.

In 1928, Ibañéz took control of the press and began ruling via executive decrees, limiting congressional independence. The models of government most mentioned in Chile during those years were those of the dictatorship of Primo de Rivera in Spain and of Fascist Italy. However, Ibañéz was not enthusiastic about the authoritarian and corporatist reform of political representation and instead retained the 1925 Constitution that just made mention of the theme. In fact, between more 'functional' or corporatist models, mixed models of trade union representation and parties, the debate about the 1925 Constitution passed through several proposals for corporatist representation, namely in the Conservative Party on the initiative of a traditionalist Catholic faction, but the results were very limited.[4]

Despite the clear influence of certain aspects of the Primo de Rivera dictatorship and the social legislation of Italian Fascism in sectors of the regime – particularly those concerned with social intervention and interest groups – being less marked by the influence of Catholic traditionalism, Ibáñez and the Chilean military were more comfortable with the parties.[5] As in other Latin American countries, the Catholic Church, social Catholicism, and Catholic trade unionists made the several versions of corporatism a central dimension of their sociopolitical activism, but their relation with the Conservative Party was not easy.[6] Some elements of the hierarchy gave voice to the corporatist appeal as well.[7]

Ibáñez was one of the first Latin American dictators to 'integrate' the working class through state 'legal' unionization, the process occurring before the 1929 world depression.[8] In 1931, his Labour Department produced a labour code which consolidated the 1924 'social legislation' of Alessandri and creating an authoritarian system of government-labour relations with and 'explicitly authoritarian, corporative orientation'.[9] He also expanded state agencies to coordinate almost all functional sectors of the economy, from industry to agriculture and fishing. After the repression of existing left-wing trade unions, he created the National Confederation of Legal Unions (CNSL – Confederación Nacional de Sindicatos Legales) and Republican Confederation for Civic Action of Workers and Employees (CRAC – Confederación Republicana de Acción Cívica de Obreros y Empleados de Chile) as the only legally authorized labour organizations, the latter being an instrument of political mobilization and of the integration into the regime of blue- and white-collar workers. A blend of corporatist institution and political party, and with parliamentary representation, CRAC served as a representative body alongside the parties in a controlled Congress. CRAC, which was founded in December 1929, may have been an embryonic dominant 'party-corporation' of Ibáñez's regime. As one of its manifestos declared, its goal was to collaborate with the government and to ensure the 'extirpation of the individual political state in order to establish the corporatist state as supreme authority in charge of regulating the national action of all the elements of which it is composed'; however, it was resisted by the parties and following a series of complex negotiations it was limited to sending fourteen deputies to Congress.[10] This party never became a central part of the political arena of the period and in any event, its existence was cut short when Ibáñez stood down as President following a wave of protest movements in 1931. His creation of a state-sponsored union movement within the framework of a highly constraining corporatist labour law did not last long either.[11]

A mixture of corporatism and socialism was present within one small party, New Public Action (NAP – Nueva Acción Pública), which was also part of a coalition government known as the Socialist Republic, that included Ibañistas, democrats and socialists. This regime was overthrown after just twelve days by one of its more conservative founders, the Ibañista Carlos Dávila, with the support of the army.[12] Proclaiming himself provisional president, Dávila dissolved the junta in early July, and proclaimed a state of siege.

Coming to power as a consequence of the crisis, outlined a series of political and economic reforms that became known as the Dávila Plan.[13] Considered a 'technocrat' or a 'planner', Dávila went much further than Ibáñez's 'flirtation with corporatism' and represented a more serious attempt to institutionalize it. In order to intervene in the economy and with interest groups along 'functional' lines, the new dictator established a consultative National Economic Council. He also planned to replace parties with corporatist political institutions, convening a constitutional assembly, in which they were already present.[14] He said:

> We want to believe that when talking about a Congress with a functional or syndicalist nature, the idea is expressed of giving the unions, within a reformed electoral law, the same prerogatives that political parties have in the presentation of candidates.[15]

In some documents, this was made clearer when he emphasized the explicit objective of opening political representation to 'the salaried employees and employer associations', all the while counting on opposition from several parties.[16] However, after just 100 days in power, the armed forces removed Dávila and organized new national elections that took place at the end of 1932. Political stability returned only with the election of Arturo Alessandri Palma to his second presidential term in October 1932.

During the 1930s, corporatism permeated strongly within several political parties and elites, ranging from conservatives to fascists, as well as important segments of the forerunners of the Chilean Christian Democratic Party. It long had a presence within the Conservative Party and at its 1932 convention, for example, the party called for an 'organic' society organized along 'functional' lines, although in a less statist manner that supported by its authoritarian counterparts. Papal encyclicals and fears of communism were ever-present in its political discourse. Corporatism was particularly evident in the youth organization that gave birth to a pro-fascist, authoritarian, and Catholic current – the Falange Nacional – of which future leaders of Chilean Christian Democracy, such as Eduardo Frei and Manuel Garretón, were members.[17] During the 1930s, authoritarian corporatism was supported by such Catholic intellectuals as Jaime Eyzaguirre whose magazine *Estudios* perhaps 'represented the maximum expression of the authoritarian-corporative project in Chile' during that decade, expressing a great deal of sympathy for the Dollfuss regime in Austria and the Salazar regime in Portugal.[18] *Estudios* was perhaps 1930 Chile's most outspoken promoter of the Portuguese New State's authoritarian corporatism. In it, they saw a 'hierarchical and corporatist regime' emerging from the ruins of liberalism.[19]

Corporatism became an important aspect in the political manifestos of such parties and movements as the Chilean National Socialist Movement (MNSC – Movimiento Nacional Socialista Chileno), the Republican Militia (MR – La Milicia Republicana), and the Agrarian Workers' Party (PAL – Partido Agrario Laborista).[20] The Spanish models were also promoted, with the MNSC being ideologically closer to the Spanish Phalange than it was to German National Socialism.[21] Another example of a corporatist project in the 1930s was that of business associations who in 1934 came together in the Confederation of Production and Commerce (CPC – Confederación de la Producción y el Comercio). There was even a short-lived Popular Corporatist Party. However, the 'professedly corporatist parties together garnered less than 10 per cent of the votes in the national congressional election of 1937'.[22] Although always present in Chilean political culture during the 1930s, authoritarian corporatism was in decline when the Popular Front brought Pedro Aguirre Cerda to the presidency in 1938, in one of the few democracies in Latin America in the inter-war period.

Notes

1 P. W. Drake, 'Corporatism and functionalism in modern Chilean politics', *Journal of Latin American Studies*, Volume 10, Number 1, 1978, p. 91.
2 On the social impact of the 1929 crisis in Chile, see A. Vergara, 'Chilean workers and the Great Depression, 1930–38', in Drinot and Knight, eds., *The Great Depression in Latin America*, pp. 51–80.
3 See M. Sznadjer, 'Nationalist authoritarianism and corporatism in Chile', in Pinto and Finchelstein, eds., *Authoritarianism and Corporatism in Europe and Latin America*, pp. 254–74.

4 E. Brahm García, 'El partido conservador frente a la crisis constitucional de 1925', *Revista Chilena de Derecho*, Volume 44, Number 1, 2017, pp. 261–85.
5 For a reference to the Portuguese military dictatorship of the late 1920s, see E. Brahm García, 'Algunos aspectos del proceso de socialización del derecho de propiedad en Chile durante el gobierno del general Carlos Ibáñez del Campo (1927–1931)', *Zitiervorschlag: Rechtsgeschichte – Legal History*, Volume 20, 2012, pp. 234–56.
6 R. Bruno-Jofré, 'The Catholic Church in Chile and the social question in the 1930s: The political pedagogical discourse of Fernando Vives del Solar, S.J', *The Catholic Historical Review*, Volume 99, Number 4, 2013, pp. 703–26.
7 See F. B. Pike, *Chile and the United States, 1880–1962: The Emergence of Chile's Social Crisis and the Challenge to United States Diplomacy*, Notre Dame, IN, University of Notre Dame Press, 1963, pp. 191–5.
8 J. Rojas Flores, *La Dictadura de Ibáñez y los Sindicatos*, Santiago de Chile, Centro de Investigaciones Diego Barros Arana, 1993.
9 B. Lovement, *Chile: The Legacy of Hispanic Capitalism*, New York, NY, Oxford University Press, 1979, pp. 250–1. Alessandri's 1924 labour law was the first such major law in Latin America, when 'there were not many models available anywhere to draw on', see Collier and Collier, *Shaping the Political Arena*, p. 193.
10 Flores, *La Dictadura de Ibáñez y los Sindicatos*, pp. 127–8.
11 P. Deshazo, *Urban Workers and Labor Uniòns in Chile, 1902–1927*, Madison, University of Wisconsin Press, 1983, p. XXIX.
12 S. S. de Groote, 'El gobierno de Carlos Dávila', *Boletín de la Academia Chilena de Historia*, Volume 62, 1995, pp. 293–360.
13 de Groote, 'El gobierno de Carlos Dávila', p. 298.
14 E. D. Palma González, 'El estado Socialista según la legislación irregular de Carlos Dávila (Junio-Septiembre de 1932)', *Estudios Constitucionales*, Volume 15, Number 1, 2017, p. 389.
15 Cit. in de Groote, 'El gobierno de Carlos Dávila', p. 322.
16 *El Mercurio*, 18 June 1932, p. 9.
17 C. Fariña Vicuña, 'Notas sobre el pensamiento corporativo de la juventud conservadora a través del periódico "Lircay" (1934–1940)', *Revista de Ciencia Política*, Volume 9, Number 1, 1987, pp. 119–42; Contreras-Vejar, 'Unorthodox fate: The rise of Chile's Christian Democratic Party', pp. 58–72; G. Gomes, 'El anticomunismo de la Juventud Conservadora Chilena: El caso de Falange Nacional (1935–1957)', *Mediações*, Volume 19, Number 1, 2014, pp. 170–86.
18 M. Luis Corvalán, 'Nacionalistas y corporativistas chilenos de la primera mitad del siglo XX', *Revista www.izquierdas.cl*, 18, IDEA-USACH, 2014, pp. 57–73. The example of Salazar's New State was ever-present in *Estudios*. See G. Vial Correa, 'El pensamiento social de Jaime Eyzaguirre', *Dimensión Histórica de Chile*, Volume 3, 1986, p. 130.
19 C. Ruiz, 'Notes on authoritarian ideologies in Chile', *NorthSouth*, Volume 6, Number 11, 1981, pp. 29–30; G. Catalán, 'Notas sobre proyectos corporativos in Chile: La revista Estudios, 1933–38'; J. J. Brunner and G. Catalán, *Cinco Estudios sobre Cultura y Sociedad*, Santiago de Chile, FLACSO, 1985, pp. 177–260.

20 E. Bohoslavsky, 'Contra el hobre de la calle: Ideas y proyetos del corporativismo católico chileno (1932–1954)', *Si Somos Americanos, Revista de Estudios Transfronterizos*, Volume VIII, Number 1, 2006, pp. 105–25.
21 M. Klein, 'The Chilean Movimiento Nacional Socialista, the German-Chilean community, and the Third Reich, 1932–1939', *The Americas*, Volume 60, Number 4, 2004, pp. 589–616; Deutsch, *Las Derechas*, pp. 143–92.
22 Drake, 'Corporatism and functionalism in modern Chilean politics', p. 98.

6 Peru under Sánchez Cerro and Benavides

When Colonel Sánchez Cerro's military coup in August 1930 overthrew Augusto Leguía, there was no real process of regime change in Peru because President Leguía had governed using dictatorial powers. Sánchez Cerro was forced to resign in 1931, only to return in the wake of presidential elections later that same year.[1] He was replaced by the conservative General Óscar Benavides (1933–39) following his assassination two years later.

The early 1930s were years of major economic and political instability in Peru due largely to the 1929 Depression, and Leguía was overthrown following violent demonstrations in Lima. The coup led by Sánchez Cerro, an old conspirator who had been exiled on several occasions, reflected the crisis of oligarchic liberalism and the entry of new social sectors into Peruvian political life. This instability was partially shaped by the formation of new more ideological 'mass' parties, such as the Peruvian Communist Party (PCP – Partido Comunista Peruano), the American Popular Revolutionary Alliance (APRA – Alianza Popular Revolucionaria Americana), and Sánchez Cerro's Revolutionary Union (UR – Unión Revolucionaria), that significantly 'expanded and polarized the political arena'.[2] During his sixteen months in office, through his minister Luis A. Flores, Sánchez Cerro used emergency laws to repress the opposition APRA.

Sánchez Cerro presented himself as a charismatic *caudillo*, and created a party, the UR, as a way to support his candidacy for President and within the new constitutional assembly. With an anti-APRA, anti-left, and nationalist discourse, in the framework of an electoral campaign marked by violence, Sánchez Cerro was elected and the UR came to dominate the constitutional assembly. The electoral platform he presented in 1931, even if overlooked by the candidate himself, 'demonstrated that the Sánchezcerristas had an essentially corporatist view of politics and society'.[3] However, his leadership, the political-electoral dynamics, and the UR received much more widespread support than any other similar dominant party-creation experiences in 1930s Latin America. In fact, with the UR fulfilling its function of ensuring Sánchez Cerro's victory and domination of the constitutional assembly, the new party incorporated an important set of clubs and popular associations in its structure, leading towards the creation of a mass party, which scholars suggest was pointing towards the establishment of a single party. However, Sánchez Cerro's assassination by an APRA activist in 1933 also brought an end to the single-party project.

It was in this context that a Catholic party, the Popular Union (UP – Unión Popular), was founded in 1931 to contest that year's elections and rapidly dissolved.[4] Both social and political corporatism were part of its political programme, but with a mixture of admiration for and demarcation from Italian fascism, which was much commented upon in the contemporary Catholic press. Associated with the programme of social Catholicism, its manifesto envisaged a Senate with corporatist representation operating alongside a chamber of deputies elected by universal suffrage.[5] The model was very close to that proposed by Víctor Andrés Belaúnde, the most important Catholic intellectual-politician of that time.[6] In one of his books, published in 1931, Belaúnde defended corporatism and his 'democracia social' contained a synthesis of liberal elements with 'functional' representation.[7]

The constitutional assembly dominated by Sánchez Cerro's UR approved a Constitution that involved corporatist representation, and which was evidence of greater support among deputies. The 1933 Constitution thus created, in its own words, a 'functional Senate' in a bicameral system and an advisory National Economic Council (CEN – Consejo de Economía Nacional). Víctor Balaúnde was one of the main contributors to this Constitution.[8] Sánchez Cerro's successor did not institutionalize this 'functional Senate', which was supposed to be elected by the regions and a corporatist vote. The CEN, which some authors claim was inspired by the Weimar Constitution, 'consisted of representatives of consumers, capital, labour and the liberal professions'.[9]

Another important intellectual-politician supporter of corporatism in the 1930s was José de la Riva-Agüero, a renowned historian and politician who in the late 1920s, after a prolong stay in Europe, abandoned liberalism to become a prominent sympathizer of Action Française and maintained close ties with the Spanish Action (AE – Acción Española).[10] He saw Mussolini as Italy's 'new Richelieu', filtered by traditionalist Catholicism and elitism.[11] Stigmatized in the APRA press as an 'erudite Sánchez Cerro', while Prime Minister to Benavides from 1933 to 1934, the aristocratic Riva-Agüero tried to institutionalize corporatism from above and supporting the UR and its black shirt militia. However, Benavides forced his resignation in May 1934.[12] In 1935, he founded Patriotic Action (AP – Acción Patriótica), the first manifestos of which outlined a clearly radical right-wing version of corporatism, that associated state economic interventionism and a corporatist political representation that no longer complemented that of liberal democracy. For this 1930s Peruvian 'modern right', corporatism was the model of the future.[13] While Riva-Agüero was an admirer of Mussolini and convinced Il Duce's model could have universal application, he recognized that the most feasible model for Latin America was the Portuguese New State 'because it was more in line with our aims and customs'.[14]

Prior to the elections of 1936, while APRA and the PCP were banned, Benavides continued to govern with the support of some of the political parties and representative institutions based on the new Constitution. Following the departure of a large number of deputies to create the Benavides supporting Nationalist Party (PN – Partido Nacionalista), it was under the leadership of Luis A. Flores, who succeeded Sánchez Cerro following the president's death, that UR adopted a more clearly fascist stance, both in terms of its structure and its political programme. The UR went on to become one of more important fascist parties in Latin America, only challenged by the Brazilian Integralist Action (AIB – Ação Integralista Brasileira), and was an important player in the political conflicts in Peru during the 1930s. In the mid-1930s, fascist corporatism became associated with UR's political programme.

While supported by certain sectors of the Benavides government, under Flores' leadership the UR made integral corporatism one of its political goals that it brandished against APRA. The UR's militia received government aid during Riva-Agüero's premiership, although the armed forces exerted pressure on the government to end this support, while Benavides became very suspicious of the party's increasing political success. Over time, the UR became a radical right-wing opposition to Benavides.

The text of the Italian Labour Charter was published in the UR newspaper *Acción* (Action) in 1934, with integral corporatism becoming the main political alternative to Benavides and APRA. As the UR stated in 1936, 'The Revolutionary Union temporarily accepts the current system of state organization, but it will fight for its evolution to an integral corporatist state, which will be possible when the technical organization of all aspects of activity coexisting within the nation are complete'.[15]

In the 1936 presidential election, Flores campaigned 'as the champion of a corporatist state in Peru, free of Marxism and subversion and to ensure social justice'.[16] In fact, in the second point of its manifesto, the UR stated that it supported: 'the gradual transformation of the present liberal democratic system to a corporatist one in which it is possible to represent all the activities of the nation perfectly' as a path towards the 'totalitarian corporatist state'.[17]

The peak of UR's presence within Peru's political landscape came in the elections of 1936, when Flores received 29.1 per cent of the vote, coming in behind Luis Antonio Eguiguren, who was the candidate supported by the banned APRA. Arguing Eguiguren was a candidate for illegal parties, Benavides declared the election null and void. With the support of some young pro-UR military officers, Flores responded to Benavides's coup with one of his own, leading to his arrest and exile, and to the banning of the UR. This led to a new period of openly dictatorial rule under Benavides, who retained a mandate from Congress until 1939.

In 1940, Víctor Balaúnde, in an overview of the Benavides regime, emphasized the three conditions open to his dictatorship: strict coercion, social reform, and organizing the *fuerzas vivas* within a functional Senate. According to Belaúnde, the Benavides regime met only two of these conditions: repression and some social reforms.[18] In fact, from 1936, Benavides suspended the 1933 Constitution and relied on the armed forces for support: he neither consolidated a single party nor introduced any alternative model of political representation.[19]

Benavides was said 'to have expressed an admiration for Italy and Mussolini, and to have raised the possibility of rewriting the Peruvian Constitution along Italian-style corporatist lines'.[20] The reports from the Italian Embassy to Rome noted that Benavides had agreed to invite Italian 'experts at the earliest possible time to study the feasibility of applying the corporative system to Peru', but the institutionalization of social corporatism was very limited.[21] Both the governments of Luis Sánchez Cerro and Óscar Benavides (following Leguía) introduced a series of 'social action' measures alongside the repression of left-wing unions.[22] Under the slogan 'order, peace and work', Benavides's discourse presented social action or corporatism as the non-partisan pursuit of social justice, employing the already classical rhetoric of a harmonious collaboration between capital and labour.[23] A rhetoric that 'resonated with Italian corporatism, so too did the rhetoric of inter-war social politics in most countries' during the 1930s.[24] The Ministry of Public Health, Labour and Social Welfare was the agent for this social strategy, and in March 1936, it promulgated a law regulating

Peru under Sánchez Cerro and Benavides 51

the legal oversight of labour affairs. While not resulting in the creation of state-controlled unions, this 'supreme decree' introduced strict controls over trade unions and workers' associations as part of a dynamic that could mean limited social corporatism from below.[25]

Benavides did not escape US suspicions that he was collaborating in the expansion of Nazism and fascism in Latin America, with Washington exerting pressure to stop it. In the eyes of Washington, Benavides was a 'poorer and poorer neighbour', who was moving Peru towards fascism[26]; however, before the US was in a position to impose more radical measures, Benavides withdrew from power. In the wake of a coup against him in 1939, Benavides planned a quick succession that would be legitimized via a manipulated electoral procedure. He abandoned the presidency following a plebiscite on some revisions of the 1933 Constitution that limited some of Congress's powers.[27]

Notes

1 For a study of this election as a form of populist mobilization, see R. S. Jansen, *Revolutionizing Repertoires: The Rise of Populist Mobilization in Peru*, Chicago, IL, University of Chicago Press, 2017.
2 P. Drinot, *The Allure of Labor: Workers, Race, and the Making of the Peruvian State*, Durham, NC, Duke University Press, 2014, p. 125.
3 *Programa de Gobierno del Comandante Luis M. Sánchez Cerro candidato a la Presidencia de la Republica del Perú*, Lima, 1931. See S. Stein, *Populismo in Perú: The Emergence of the Masses and the Politics of Social Control*, Madison, University of Wisconsin Press, 1980, p. 112.
4 J. Klaiber, 'Los partidos católicos en el Perú', *Historica*, Volume VII, Number 2, 1983, p. 163; R. D. C. Ramacciotti, *The Politics of Religion and the Rise of Social Catholicism in Peru (1884–35)*, Leiden, Brill, 2018, pp. 87–9.
5 *Verdades*, 31 January 1931, p. 1. See P. Planas, *Biografía del Movimiento Social-Cristiano en el Perú (1926–1956): Apuntes*, Lima, Faculdad de Teología Pontificia y Civil de Lima, 1996.
6 V. A. Belaúnde, T. G. Lima and S. A. Villanueva, *El Debate Constitucional: Discursos en la Asamblea, 1931–32*, Lima, La Tradicion, 1966, pp. 83–90.
7 V. A. Belaúnde, *La Realidad Nacional*, Paris, Editorial "Le Livre Libre", 1931.
8 J. Klaiber, *La Iglesia en el Perú: Su Historia Social desde la Independencia*, Lima, Fondo Editorial de la Pontificia Universidad Católica del Perú, 1988, p. 325.
9 Article 182 of the Constitution of 1933. Haya de la Torre and APRA was a proponent of a *congreso económico*, inspired by the Weimar Constitution. See F. J. Eguiguren Praeli, 'El desarollo del proceso político constitucional en Perú', in C. Andrews, ed., *Un Siglo de Constitucionalismo en América Latina*, Mexico City, CIDE, 2017, p. 417.
10 According to V. S. Rivera, 'In 1936, with the blessing of Maurras, the Marquis de Montealegre founded his own Peruvian branch, Action Patriotique, a Peruvian version of Action Française', see his 'Charles Maurras et Montealegre:

Un marquis péruvien face aux Empires 1913–14', *Rivista Elettronica della Società Italiana di Filosofia Politica*, undated, p. 21. See also F. Bobadilla, 'José de La Riva-Agüero y Osma o el intelectual antimoderno', *Revista Mercurio Peruano*, Volume 520, 2007, pp. 46–81.
11 J. Vásquez Benavides, 'Lo constante en el ideario politico de José de la Riva-Agüero', *Boletin del Instituto Riva-Agüero*, Volume 21, 1994, p. 257. For an anthology of many of the Peruvian admirers of fascism see, *El Pensamiento Fascista (1930–1945): Selección y Prólogo de José Ignacio López Soria*, Lima, Mosca Azul, 1981.
12 E. González Calleja, 'La derecha latinoamericana en busca de un modelo fascista: La limitada influencia del falangismo en el Perú (1936–45)', *Revista Complutense de Historia de América*, Volume 20, 1994, p. 236.
13 E. Candela, 'La Acción Patriótica: Un movimiento doctrinario en una época polarizada (1935–36)', *Elecciones*, Volume 10, Number 11, 2011, p. 186.
14 J. de la Riva-Agüero, *Obras Completas*, Vol. Xl, Lima, Pontificia Universidad Catolica del Perú, 1975, p. 291.
15 Cit. in Morales, *La Unión Revolucionaria, 1931–39*, 2004, p. 265.
16 O. Ciccarelli, 'Fascism and politics in Peru during the Benavides regime, 1933–39: The Italian perspective', *The Hispanic American Historical Review*, Volume 70, Number 3, 1990, p. 414.
17 *El Comercio*, 14 July 1936, p. 12, cit. in Morales, *La Unión Revolucionaria*, p. 451.
18 E. I. Candela Jiménez, 'El régimen de Óscar R. Benavides (1933–1939): Una experiencia populista? Definiciones y nuevos planteamientos en torno a su accionar político', master's thesis, Lima, Pontificia Universidad Catolica del Perú, 2013, p. 197; V. A. Belaúnde, *El Debate Constitucional*, Lima, Comisión Nacional del Centenario de Víctor Andrés Belaúnde, 1987, p. 396.
19 For a definition of the Benavides dictatorship as 'military-autocratic', see T. A. Molinari Morales, 'Dictadura, cultura autoritaria y conflicto político en el Perú, 1936–39', doctoral thesis, Lima, Universidad Nacional Mayor de San Marcos, 2012, p. 104.
20 Ciccarelli, 'Fascism and politics in Peru', pp. 417–18.
21 Ibid., p. 418.
22 R. J. Alexander, *A History of Organized Labor in Peru and Ecuador*, Westport, CT, Praeger, 2007.
23 *Mensaje presentado al Congreso del Perú por el señor General de División don Óscar R. Benavides, Presidente Constitucional de la República*, Lima, 1939, p. 111.
24 Drinot, *The Allure of Labor*, pp. 126–7.
25 P. Drinot, 'Fighting for a closed shop: The 1931 Lima bakery workers' strike', *Journal of Latin American Studies*, Volume 35, 2003, pp. 249–78.
26 Ciccarelli, 'Fascism and politics in Peru', p. 427.
27 T. A. Molinari Morales, 'La dictadura militar-autocrática de Benavides y la instrumentalizada coyuntura electoral de 1939', *Investigaciones Sociales*, Volume 15, Number 27, 2011, pp. 349–68.

7 Rafael Franco and the 'Febrerista' regime in Paraguay

In Paraguay, on the other side of the 1932–35 Chaco War, the overthrow of President Eusebio Ayala following the military victory over Bolivia, ended 32 years of liberal order with the non-hierarchical military coup of February 1936 that invited the nationalist Colonel Rafael Franco to head the new government.[1] The new regime exiled General José Félix Estigarribia Insaurralde, who was head of the Paraguayan armed forces. Although it had a loose programme that was initially supported by the left, nationalism was the ideology that bound Febrerismo together.[2]

Decree-Law No. 152, which was to be a preliminary blueprint for the 'political content [...] of the liberating revolution' provided for the calling of a national constitutional assembly that would be charged with determining the 'definitive modern organization of the republic'.[3] Nevertheless, the identification of the new regime with the global authoritarian wave of the 1930s was clear.[4] The decree stated that the new regime was aligned with the 'totalitarian social transformations in contemporary Europe, in the sense that the liberating revolution and the state are one and the same thing'.[5] Meanwhile, all political activity was prohibited for a period of one year in order to allow space for the creation of new political institutions.

The ministerial elite of the first Franco cabinet included Juan Stefanich, leader of the National Independent League (LNI – Liga Nacional Independiente) and one of the leading intellectual-politicians preaching support for a 'solidarist democracy' based on an 'organic' view of society.[6] Stefanich firmly believed the introduction of corporatism could be applied advantageously to Paraguay as a sort of 'authentic Paraguayan doctrine'.[7] He helped organize the Febrerista revolt, hoping to make the LNI the backbone of Franco's official party. He was appointed Minister of Foreign Affairs and became an important ideologist of a new regime that included a very disparate and politically contradictory elite.[8]

Another member of Franco's first ministry was Freire Esteves, a former liberal who had become influenced by fascism and who was appointed Minister of the Interior where he had responsibility for social affairs. The Minister of Agriculture, Bernardino Caballero, was closer to German political culture. He was the main author of the May 1936 agrarian reform law that provided for the expropriation of land on payment of an indemnity to the former owners and for the creation of small and medium farms.[9] Nevertheless, the cabinet was politically diverse and other members were both suspicious and openly critical of these pro-fascist ministers.

Gomes Freire Esteves was initially given complete control over labour and industrial relations, under the guidance of a national labour department. He wrote Franco's first proclamations and played the role of the cabinet 'strongman' who would provide clear content to Franco's project to build a new 'organic democracy' in Paraguay.[10] One of the new government's first measures was to introduce Paraguay's first labour code in a document that was heavily inspired by the Italian Labour Charter.[11] Existing unions were given official status as the state-controlled Paraguay Workers' Confederation (CPT – Confederacion Paraguaya de Trabajadores) was established to replace the National Workers' Confederation (CNT – Confederacion Nacional de Trabajadores) that had been dismantled by the government. As in many other processes of corporatist reorganization of the union movement, all labour organizations were forced to obtain legal recognition from the Department of Labour, which was responsible for 'regulating the solidarity and cooperation between producers'.[12] At the same time, some social rights were introduced, including the eight-hour day, annual paid holidays, and one day off a week.[13]

While tensions within the government and the reaction of labour to state intervention and repression of the union movement led to the resignation of the pro-fascist Freire Esteves, the attempt to create a single party was also a major divisive factor. The creation of the National Revolutionary Party (PNR – Partido Nacional Revolucionario) as the first political support base for the new regime failed almost immediately with the imprisonment of the CNT's leader, Francisco Gaona. Its declaration of principles included 'representative and functional democracy as an organizing system'.[14] Stefanich, who had emerged as the new *éminence grise* of the regime and strong man of the cabinet, was the main figure behind the creation of the National Revolutionary Union (UNR – Unión Nacional Revolucionaria) as the new regime's official party in November 1936, becoming its first President. Founded at the invitation of Rafael Franco, already without *Febrerismo*'s 'left-wing', the UNR would have a more conservative base, with the organizational structure of the National Association of Former Combatants (ANEC – Asociación Nacional de Ex-Combatientes) and the political and ideological leadership of the LNI of Stefanich, author of its declaration of principles.[15] In a message to the nation celebrating the first year of the revolution, Rafael Franco, whose discourse was 'neither extreme right nor extreme left', claimed the UNR had a new historical mission to consolidate his regime, which was all the more important given the regime intended to elect a National Constituent Convention.[16] Stefanich had conversations with some political parties in which he tried to convince them to join this official party, but the Colorado Party was firmly opposed to its creation. The party had not developed, since the February Revolution government was overthrown by a liberal-inspired coup within eighteen months, but much of the social legislation survived.

In August 1937, Supreme Court judge Félix Paiva replaced Franco as provisional president after a military intervention that had the support of some political parties. Sometime later a faction of the Liberal Party nominated General Estigarribia for the position of president in a complex election. The General proclaimed himself dictator in 1940, while promising to restore a legitimate government with a new Constitution in which some of Franco's corporatist projects were included. At the same time, the *Tiempo* group of corporatist Catholic intellectual-politicians organized around the newspaper of the same name, became influential. This group looked beyond Mussolini towards the authoritarian political regimes on the Iberian Peninsula as their reference. One of its leaders claimed the Catholic and corporatist Portuguese New State of Oliveira Salazar was the model 'we looked to'.[17] The *Tiempistas* initially supported Estigarribia, while remaining somewhat suspicious of the inclusion of Liberal Party members into his government.

The new Constitution was published on 10 July 1940 and was ratified by a plebiscite. Unlike its predecessor of 1870, it granted the state the right to 'regulate national economic life'. 'Under no circumstance', it proclaimed, 'will private interests prevail over the nation's general interests': private property would be respected only if it served a useful social function".[18] The preamble, signed by Estigarribia, was clear: 'provide the state with faculties enabling it more broadly to ensure progress and to intervene to achieve greater social justice, guide the economy, rationalize production and systematize national labour'.[19] Congress was made unicameral and its powers limited, while those of the president were expanded to include the power to dissolve parliament and rule by decree. In an effort to emulate other corporatist institutions, a council of state comprising ministers and representatives of farmers' organizations, livestock industries, businessmen, the armed forces, the university, and the Catholic Church, was created as an advisory body.

Estigarribia died in air crash in September 1940, and his successor, Higinio Morínigo, resumed the alliance with the *Tiempistas*, quickly proclaiming the new regime's motto: Order, Discipline, and Hierarchy.[20] This traditionist Catholic group gave Morínigo ideological and political support, and its main leader Luis Argaña was appointed Minister of Foreign Affairs. The new dictator also moved closer to the *Febreristas*, although he did so more for reasons of propaganda than for pursuing the institutional contents of the 1936 projects. When the US and the turn in the tide of the Second World War away from the Axis forced Morínigo to liberalize his regime, the dynamics of inter-war institutional change was already partly over.

Notes

1. P. H. Lewis, *Political Parties and Generations in Paraguay's Liberal Era, 1869–1940*, Chapel Hill, University of North Carolina Press, 1993.
2. P. R. Caballero Cáceres, 'La instauración del nacionalismo como política de Estado durante el gobierno del Coronel Rafael Franco (1936–1937)', *Trans-Pasando Fronteras*, Volume 7, 2015, pp. 151–78.
3. See the English version of the first proclamation of the coup in F. W. Smith and C. Recalde, 'Proclamation of the Febrerista Revolution', in P. Lambert and A. Nickson, eds., *The Paraguay Reader: History, Culture, Politics*, London, Routledge, 2012, pp. 216–19.
4. See this and other documents of the Franco period in A. M. Seiferheld, *Nazismo y Fascismo en el Paraguay: Vísperas de la II Guerra Mundial, 1936–1939*, Asunción, Editorial Histórica, 1983, pp. 211–24.
5. Seiferheld, Ibid., p. 215.
6. See H. Caballero Campos, *Juan Stefanich: Canciller de la Revolución*, Asunción, El Lector, 2011.
7. Cit. in H. G. Warren, 'Political aspects of the Paraguayan revolution, 1936–1940', *Hispanic American Historical Review*, Volume 30, February 1950, p. 13. For Stefanich, the goal was the creation of a government in which individuals and the groups to which they belong – being naturally interdependent – will live harmoniously, since 'he is a member of a family, a municipality, a race, a nation, a region, a continent, and of humanity'. See J. Stefanich, *El Paraguay Nuevo: Por la Democracia y la Libertad Hacia un Nuevo Ideario Americano*, Buenos Aires, Editorial Claridad, 1943, p. 106.
8. Stefanich later came to reject authoritarian corporatist ideology. See P. Lewis, *The Politics of Exile: Paraguay's Febrerista Party*, Chapel Hill, University of North Carolina Press, 1968.
9. 'Paraguay since 1930', p. 237.
10. Lewis, *Political Parties and Generations*, p. 162.

11 Seiferheld, *Nazismo y Fascismo en el Paraguay*, p. 42. Lewis, *Political Parties and Generations*, p. 164.
12 See the decree-law that created it in F. Gaona, *Introducción à la Historia Gremial y Social del Paraguay*, Vol. 3, Asunción, Centro de Documentación y Estudios, 1990, pp. 50–3.
13 'Paraguay since 1930', p. 237.
14 R. Céspedes Ruffinelli, *El Febrerismo: Del Movimiento al Partido, 1936–1951*, Asunción, Arandurã Editorial, 2013, p. 58.
15 See the founding act in Appendix 1, Ruffinelli, *El Febrerismo*, p. 144.
16 *Mensaje al pueblo del presidente provisional de la República del Paraguay Coronel Rafael Franco, 17 de Febrero de 1937, primer aniversario de la revolución libertadora*, Asunción, Imprenta Nacional, 1937, p. 5.
17 Cit. in Seiferheld, *Nazismo y Fascismo en Paraguay*, p. 181. See also M. Grow, *The Good Neighbor Policy and Authoritarianism in Paraguay: United States Economic Expansion and Great-Power Rivalry in Latin America during World War*, Lawrence, KS, University Press of Kansas, 1981, p. 50.
18 *Constitution of the Republic of Paraguay of 1940*, Washington, DC, Pan American Union, 1963, p. 2.
19 'Constitución de Paraguay de 1940', in M. Ángel Pangrazio, ed., *Las Constituciones del Paraguay*, Asunción, Intercontinental Editora, 2010. Available at portalguarani.com/690_miguel_angel_pangrazio/13204_constitucion_de_ 1940_compilador_miguel_angel_pangrazio_ciancio_.html.
20 C. Gómez Florentín, *Higino Morínigo*, Asunción, Editorial El Lector, 2011.

8 The Bolivia of David Toro
'Military socialism' with
a fascist overtone

In the case of Bolivia, it was defeat in the 1932–35 Chaco War with Paraguay that resulted in the 17 May 1936 coup, when colonels David Toro and Germán Busch took over the government, bringing about the fall of oligarchic liberalism. Both had already participated in conspiracies and coups, but this time they finally replaced a civilian president in power. The coup marked the start of a period of political dominance by veteran officers of the Chaco War.

Once in power, both Colonel David Toro (1936–37) and then Colonel Germán Busch (1937–39) 'combined progressive state labour policies that emulated European fascism' in their efforts to create a corporatist regime based on functional representation.[1] Legitimized on a new 'social constitutionalism' for Bolivia, Toro proclaimed himself the leader of a 'military socialist revolution'.[2] In Toro's 52-point programme for immediate action, published on 25 May, the obligatory unionization, state welfare, and functional representation to replace liberal democracy was almost immediately associated with the influence of Italian Fascism within the new government.[3]

The 1930s authoritarian intellectual arena in Bolivia did not differ much from the others in Latin America, but its ideological and political diversity after the 1936 coup was more striking. Between social Catholicism, fascism, and regenerating socialism and national socialism, these networks of non-conformist intellectuals had as their common denominator new forms of organic representation that expressed the corporatist option – as in Argentina – through the functional democracy formula that included the end of political parties, and their replacement by representatives of unions and entrepreneurs.[4] While their inspiration was less marked by the radical-right than elsewhere, the first institutional steps taken by the new regime were inspired, in part, by the model suggested out by some of these non-conformists as a way of representing the combatant nation of the 1932–35 war 'through a corporatist system that surpassed parliamentary and partisan representation'.[5] On 27 July 1936, Colonel Toro said the political system had to be completely reorganized and that it was necessary to move towards a functioning parliament based on a double representation: party representation by means of direct suffrage; and a representation of interests organized in corporations.[6]

One of the first measures the new regime took was to begin the institutionalization of social corporatism. According to the Toro government, the law on mandatory trade union membership meant a 'new system for the exercise of citizenship', with political rights based in union membership and location in national production. The first Article of the decree of August 1936 obliged everyone to join a union, 'whatever their role in the production, distribution or use of wealth', and the employers as well as the workers were forced to organize themselves into these new unions.[7] Although the labour unions were autonomous, they were obliged to form mixed bodies with the employers whenever it was necessary to reach agreements between capital and labour. In short no political rights without union membership.[8] These new state-led social structures would be 'the base for the functional Constitution of the public powers' (Article 3).[9] The attempt to replace party representation with that of organized interests was followed by the creation of the Permanent National Assembly of Trade Union Organizations (Asamblea Nacional Permanente de Organizaciones Sindicales), that was to provide the structure for a new system of representation through those unions that were recognized by the government and through mandatory union membership.[10] In this way, state-sponsored unions were integrated into an umbrella organization linking labour groups with state institutions. The Minister of Labour claimed this system was attractive to the military because of the success of the Mussolini experience in Italy.[11]

While, in the face of the adverse reaction by the parties, Toro denied the aim of mandatory union membership legislation was to dissolve the political parties, the truth is that the law stated that union organization were the base for the functional organization of the new political system, suggesting that future political parties would have to be based on unions and interest organizations.[12] In fact, a government statement was clear about the political effects of mandatory unionization by when it stated that 'the union organization will include both the employers and the workers and employees [...] substituting in the political field the citizen – that abstract body of democracy – for the real man, the worker, the employee, the landowner and the capitalist'.[13]

In the meantime, the project was being criticized by both the right and by left-wing trade unionists who were fearful of state control.[14]

Toro had visited fascist Italy and 'may have aspired to replicate aspects of its Fascist state'.[15] Nevertheless, Toro preferred to claim the establishment of a functional democracy was the main goal of his plans for the new Bolivia.[16] However, if he had enough power to propose a corporatist model for parliament and forced unionization under state control, opposition from political elites supporting Toro and his pragmatism were sufficient to partially delay some of these plans. In the midst of an instable relationship with the political parties and between the military of the new regime, Toro still tried to create a dominant party, the Socialist Party of the State (PSE – Partido Socialista del Estado) to strengthen his control of the new political system and especially his dependence on the military.[17] The Minister of the Presidency, Lieutenant-Colonel Julio Viera, and other ministers travelled the length and breadth of the country to show their support for this new party, putting pressure on civil servants to join; however, the overthrow of Toro by Busch resulted in the collapse of this embryonic official government party.[18]

While reaffirming his intention to return Bolivia to political normalcy, Busch took up some of Toro's projects, including giving interest organizations the same representative status as political parties and attempted to create a government party.[19] His first declarations seemed to follow Toro's corporatist projects although abandoning the PSE and allowing the resurface of former political parties. Under his rule, in 1938 a six-month constitutional convention drafted what many described a corporatist constitution, even if it did not imply a total break with liberalism.[20] In fact, it included principles of social corporatism, but the planned bicameral system did not introduce corporatist representation. Although presented at the constitutional convention, the statist corporatist projects of Toro's Constitutional Commission, 'strongly influenced by German-Italian ideas', were not fully endorsed by a convention partially constituted by functional representation.[21] At the convention, several fascist-oriented deputies submitted proposals for corporatist representation, but the 1938 Constitution rejected them to become, after the Mexican Constitution of 1917, the most 'social' of 1930s Latin American constitutions.[22] The parties were not abolished until 1939, when Busch cancelled the elections and suspended his own Constitution. His sudden death in August 1939 prevented the consolidation of his dictatorship. In 1940, a coalition of political parties chose his successor, but the consolidation of social legislation, which came from Toro but which was now known as the 'Busch Code', survived.

Notes

1 L. Gotkowitz, *A Revolution for Our Rights: Indigenous Struggles for Land and Justice in Bolivia, 1880–1952*, Durham, NC, Duke University Press, p. 112.
2 F. Gallego, *Los Orígenes del Reformismo Militar en América Latina: La Gestión de David Toro en Bolivia (1936–1937)*, Barcelona, PPU, 1991.
3 H. S. Klein, *Parties and Political Change in Bolivia, 1880–1952*, Cambridge, Cambridge University Press, 1969, p. 235.
4 See P. Stefanoni, *Los Inconformistas del Centenario: Intelectuales, Socialismo y Nación en una Bolivia en Crisis, 1925–1939*, La Paz, Plural, 2015.
5 Gallego, 'La posguerra del Chaco en Bolivia', p. 37.
6 F. Gallego, 'Un caso de populismo militar latinoamericano: La gestions de David Toro in Bolivia, 1936–1937', *Iberoamerikanisches Archiv, Neue Folge*, Volume 14, Number 4, 1988, p. 487.
7 Cit. in G. Lora, *A History of Bolivia Labour Movement*, Cambridge, Cambridge University Press, 1977, p. 178. As Lora stresses, 'The measures referred to here show that Toro's military government made the most resolute attempt to establish fascism that the country has ever seen. What is remarkable is that some intellectuals and politicians who considered themselves to be Marxists cooperated in these endeavours', p. 180.
8 Gotkowitz, *A Revolution for our Rights*, p. 113.
9 Lora, *A History of Bolivia Labour Movement*, p. 179.
10 Gallego, 'La posguerra del Chaco en Bolivia', p. 38.
11 Cit. in Gallego, Ibid., p. 38.
12 H. S. Klein, 'David Toro and the establishment of "military socialism" in Bolivia', *The Hispanic American Historical Review*, Volume 45, Number 1, 1965, p. 42.
13 Gallego, 'Un caso de populismo militar', p. 488.
14 P. Stefanoni, 'Rejuvenecer (y salvar) la nación: El socialismo militar boliviano revisitado', *Tinkazos*, Volume 18, Number 37, 2015, p. 52.
15 Gotkowitz, *Revolution for our Rights*, p. 112.
16 Klein, 'David Toro', pp. 42–3.
17 Klein, *Parties and Political Change in Bolivia*, pp. 263–4.
18 J. M. Malloy, 'Authoritarianism and corporatism: The case of Bolivia', in Malloy, ed., *Authoritarianism and Corporatism in Latin America*, p. 88.
19 H. S. Klein, 'Germán Busch and the era of "military socialism" in Bolivia', *Hispanic American Historical Review*, Volume 47, Number 2, 1967, pp. 170, 173.
20 Gotkowitz, *A Revolution for our rights*, pp. 101–2.
21 H. S. Klein, '"Social constitutionalism" in Latin America: The Bolivian experience of 1938', *The Americas*, Volume 22, Number 3, 1966, pp. 267.
22 Bolivia: *Constitución Política de 1938*, 30 October 1938.

9 Gabriel Terra and the Uruguayan *Dictablanda*

While present in the political culture of the radical-right and in some parties during the 1930s, the hybrid regime of Gabriel Terra (1932–38) and his successor, Alfredo Baldomir (1938–42), consecrated corporatism in the institutions in a very limited way.[1] Although there have been several proposals in the debates leading to the promulgation of the 1934 Constitution, in the Uruguayan case the rejection of authoritarian corporatism was more explicit, and carried out in the name of party pluralism and citizenship.

Uruguay experienced one of the most complete democratization processes during the early decades of the twentieth century, to become one of Latin America's few democracies, with a polity that was based on widespread political participation and enlightened political parties. The myth of democratic Uruguay, as a Latin American version of Switzerland, as it was described at the time, was not entirely unfounded.[2]

Gabriel Terra, a member of the Colorado Party, won the presidential elections in 1931. Two years later, on 31 March 1933, he led a coup that overthrew the National Administration Council (CAN – Consejo Nacional de Administración) that formed a dual executive system with the President of Republic, and assumed dictatorial powers. The political consequences of the 1929 crisis and pressure from conservative interest groups were clearly associated with the presidential coup while also mediated by organized tendencies within the main parties.

While the authoritarian nature of the regime following Terra's coup was clear and the establishment of censorship, the exile of some members of the opposition, and the repression of others was a fact, many contemporary observers considered it to be a *dictablanda* rather than *dictadura*. While some elements within the armed forces and supporters of the Primo de Rivera or fascist models plotted against the political system, Terra led the coup from his position as president using only the police, which was led by his brother-in-law and successor Alfredo Baldomir. In fact, 'the parties were the protagonists of the coup and were not displaced either by pressure groups or by the armed forces'.[3] Based on an alliance between the Terra and Herrera factions in the Colorado and National parties, this was reflected in the composition of the regime's political institutions, which were reserved for the two dominant party factions. As several authors note, even at times of censorship and police repression against organizations opposed to the Terra's government, as was the case with the 1935 revolt, party pluralism did not disappear.[4]

While present in Uruguayan political culture since the beginning of the century, it was only during Terra's regime that the corporatist option entered the public sphere and its political system. Corporatist alternatives were evident both through the development of radical right-wing politico-ideological groups, by the emergence of new parties with corporatist political programmes and in the framework of proposals the main parties presented at the third constitutional convention that gave rise to the 1934 Constitution.

The associational corporatism that was close to social Catholicism was disseminated by the Catholic parties, such as the Uruguay Civic Union (UCU – Unión Cívica del Uruguay), during the 1910s. One of its main ideologues, Tomás G. Brena, was a critic of the corporatist statism promoted by fascism, although he did not move away from other European and Latin American counterparts, especially from Salazar and Dollfuss.[5] A more authoritarian Catholic dissent was expressed in the *El Democrata* newspaper, which in 1933 proposed a constitutional project that would create a 'legislature composed of *a chamber of guild representatives* in such a way that all corporations are represented in a proportional and qualified manner'.[6] Brena and the UCU, however, were critical of the Axis and were active promoters of social corporatist structures, like the so-called 'Brena report' of 1940, which was produced by a parliamentary commission with neo-corporatist social concertation proposals.[7]

It was within the National and Colorado parties that the introduction of interest representation gained some popularity, where it was associated with being complementary to political representation in the early 1930s, as can be seen in the 1934 Constitution. Terra legitimized his regime with a new Constitution and the third national constitutional convention discussed several projects, including the corporatist reform of the political system.

One of the first projects, which was presented by a Colorado Party deputy, proposed the creation of a corporatist assembly, consisting of 150 members 'of an apolitical and honourable character, who would represent the guilds of production, industry, commerce and national culture'.[8] The Catholic UCU suggested a Senate partially occupied by corporatist representation.[9] The remaining projects were more moderate, providing only for the existence of an Economic Council of the Republic (CER – Consejo Económico de la República) or an advisory economic council. The commission responsible for the final project rejected some aspects of the more authoritarian institutional engineering of the projects presented. In its final report, the commission stated that, 'in Uruguay, where democratic ideals are deeply rooted among the citizenry, it is clearly impossible to speak of establishing a corporatist government as seen in other countries'. It added that it 'believes it is unthinkable that the Uruguayan state not be democratic and republican, with power achieved by means of universal suffrage'.[10]

The 1934 Constitution adopted more moderate proposals and created a Council for the National Economy, 'of a consultative and honorary nature and which was made up of representatives of the nation's economic and professional interests. The law will determine the form of its Constitution and functions'.[11] As a Uruguayan scholar noted in 1947, Uruguay adopted 'a system of subordinate corporatism, reserving the full power of decision to the bodies created by popular suffrage'.[12] The new Constitution was approved by little more than half the electorate, with factions within both parties abstaining. In his closing speech to the Constitution Convention, Terra did not mention the words functional or corporatism.[13]

Several intellectuals-politicians and parties defended and disseminated the authoritarian models and political programmes of the Uruguayan radical-right throughout the 1930s, and as for many others at that time: 'the most important novelty was the incorporation of the corporatist regime. Corporatism was what the radical-right considered to be fascism's most revolutionary innovation and as a revolutionary alternative to the party system'.[14] The most persistent in this view were Adolfo Agorio and Varela de Andrade, founders of the magazine *Corporaciones* in 1935, who in 1937 created Revisionist Action of Uruguay (RAU – Acción Revisionista del Uruguay), which became an organized tendency of the Colorado Party. In 1932, before and shortly after the coup, Varela de Andrade made an unsuccessful appeal to the Colorado Party leadership to create a 'system of corporatist parliamentary governance'.[15] Varela returned to the subject in 1938, by referring to the 1937 Constitution of Getúlio Vargas' New State in neighbouring Brazil. The AIB and its leaders, from Plínio Salgado to Gustavo Barroso, were also mentioned. Standing closer to the anti-democratic proposals of integral corporatism, they moderated their anti-party radicalism when they joined the Colorado Party. Another party that made corporatism an important element of its political programme was the Rural Party (PR – Partido Ruralista), which was formed in 1936 to represent rural interests. However, it was also far from supporting integral corporatism. The introduction of social corporatism, like the establishment of a Higher Labour Council (Consejo Superior de Trabajo), was not implemented and other projects for state control of the unions were not approved by Congress.[16] Although suffering some repression, the union movement was not integrated through corporatist-type state intervention and maintained its independence.[17] At the same time, party mediation rather than corporatist institutions was the main channel for employers' associations.[18]

Some aspects of Terra's foreign policy during the 1930s suggested he had some sympathy for European fascism in Europe. In 1935, Terra cut off relations with both the Soviet Union and the Spanish Republic, and moved closer, commercially, to Italy and Germany. Italian Fascist leader Luigi Federzoni visited the country in 1937 and reported back to Mussolini with an optimistic version of the possible penetration of fascism in this small country with a large community of Italian immigrants; however, this optimism was soon shown to be exaggerated.[19] As in other Latin American countries, several clearly fascist groups and even Nazi sympathizers were emerging, but by the late 1930s, almost all groups and parties with Fascist and Nazi sympathies were targeted and faced repression.[20] In Uruguay during the 1930s, such groups were a lot less significant than their equivalents in Brazil or Peru, for example. In the end, Terra declared his sympathy for US President Roosevelt's New Deal by stating he was for 'neither Rome nor Moscow'.[21]

In 1938, Terra was replaced by his brother-in-law, Afredo Baldomir, who removed some of the more repressive aspects of the Terra period and developed an electoral-institutional way out while realigning with the Allies and the US.[22]

Gabriel Terra's authoritarian regime knew anti-system parties that were closer to the radical-right and were powerful advocates of corporatism as well as others that were more moderate, however, the resilience of the main parties was important. From this perspective, few official documents associated with authoritarian regimes in the 1930s could be as clear as that of the 1934 Constitution Commission, which stated: 'The political task must be the exclusive responsibility of political bodies. For the commission, the only body that has the right to make laws in a true democracy is the legislature. Politicians are the best technicians in politics'.[23]

Notes

1 As the Colliers wrote 'In dealing with its opponents in the traditional party system, rather than making extensive use of repression, the Terra government depended more on constitutional changes and innovations in electoral rules'. Collier and Collier, *Shaping the Political Arena*, p. 446. See J. Lanzaro, *Sindicatos y Sistema Político: Relaciones Corporativas en el Uruguay, 1940–1985*, Montevideo, Fundación de Cultura Universitaria, 1986.
2 On the right during this period, see M. B. San Martín, 'Conformación social y caracterización ideológica de las derechas uruguayas en los años veinte', in E. Bohoslavsky, D. Jorge and C. E. Lida, eds., *Las Derechas Ibero-Americanas entre la Gran Guerra y la Gran Depresión*, Mexico City, El Colegio de México, 2019.
3 A. Alpini, *La Derecha Política en Uruguay en la Era del Fascismo, 1930–1940*, Montevideo, Fundación de Cultura Universtaria, 2015, p. 12.
4 C. R. da Rosa Rangel, 'A participação político-partidária no Uruguai e no Brasil (1930–1938)', *Historia Social*, Volume 13, 2007, p. 53.
5 T. G. Brena, *Corporativismo de Asociación*, Montevideo, Mosca Hermanos, 1937, pp. 178–94.
6 *Proyecto constitucional de El Demócrata. Implantación del régimen corporativo*, Montevideo, Talleres Gráficos "El Demócrata", 1933. Cit. in Alpini, *La Derecha Política en Uruguay*, p. 19.
7 Lanzaro, *Sindicatos y Sistema Político*, p. 48.
8 Alpini, *La Derecha Política en Uruguay*, p. 75.
9 Lanzaro, *Sindicatos y Sistema Político*, p. 44.
10 Cit. in Alpini, *La Derecha Política en Uruguay*, p. 77.
11 *Constitucion de la Republica Oriental de Uruguay de 1934*, p. 101.
12 A. Ramón Real, *El Consejo de la Economía Nacional*, Montevideo, 1947, cit. in Alpini, *La Derecha Política en Uruguay*, p. 77. Nevertheless, illustrating a more 'important development of Uruguayan corporatism' compared with its Argentinian counterpart. See O. Inés Echeverría, 'Las derechas de Argentina y Uruguay en tiempos de nazi fascismos: Radicalización, redefiniciones e influencias', *Oficina do Historiador*, Volume 9, Number 1, 2016, p. 166.
13 G. Terra, *La Revolución de Marzo*, Buenos Aires, M. Gleizer, 1938, pp. 123–8.
14 Alpini, *La Derecha Política en Uruguay*, p. 18.
15 Ibid., p. 8.
16 O. Cures, ed., *El Uruguay de los Años Treinta: Enfoques y Problemas*, Montevideo, Ediciones de la Banda Oriental, 1994, p. 151.
17 R. J. Alexander, *A History of Organized Labor in Uruguay and Paraguay*, Westport, CT, Praeger, 2005, pp. 28–30.
18 Lanzaro, *Sindicatos y Sistema Politica*, p. 46.
19 P. Carusi, 'El fascismo en Uruguay: Un testimonio de Luigi Federzoni', *Historia Actual Online*, Volume 38, Number 3, 2015, pp. 177–87. See also A. M. Rodríguez Ayçaguer, *Un Pequeño Lugar Bajo el Sol*, Montevideo, Ediciones de la Banda Oriental, 2009.
20 On the penetration of the Spanish Falange in Uruguay, see C. Zubillaga, *Una Historia Silenciada: Presencia y Acción del Falangismo en Uruguay (1936–1955)*, Montevideo, Ediciones Cruz del Sur, 2015.

21 Cit. in Lanzaro, *Sindicatos y Sistema Político*, p. 45.
22 E. Bohoslavsky, 'Los liberalismos de Argentina, Brasil y Uruguay ante el enigma peronista (1943–1955)', *Nuevo Mundo Mundos Nuevos*, available at nuevomundo.revues.org/68805.
23 *Diario de Sesiones de la Convención Nacional Constituyente*, Vol. II, 16 March 1934, p. 185.

10 The New State of Getúlio Vargas
The primacy of social corporatism in Brazil

The New State established in Brazil by Getúlio Vargas (1937–45) is the most important case of the institutionalization of corporatism in an authoritarian setting in Latin America. While corporatist representation was outlined in the 1937 Constitution, social corporatism had a durable legacy and Vargas's dictatorship represented a much more powerful break with political liberalism than was the case with other contemporary regimes in Latin America. On the other hand, in Brazil the diffusion of corporatism was more developed in conservative and fascist political circles and movements and as a proposed reform of political representation within a liberal framework. In fact, from the beginning of the 1930s, several important steps towards the institutionalization of social corporatism had been taken, and the representation of interests institutionalized in the 1934 constitutional assembly and later consolidated with the New State in 1937.

The 1930 Revolution opened the crisis of the old republic's oligarchic liberalism in Brazil and launched a complex political process marked by a great deal of political instability prior to the 1937 coup.[1] Mobilizing junior officers, the so-called *tenentes*, some high-ranking officials, favouring a more centralized and efficient state by dismantling the clientelistic political structures of the old republic and its regional political parties, the political forces that came to power with Getúlio Vargas in November 1930 were more heterogeneous than was the case with other similar processes in Latin America. Nevertheless, one of the main promises of the provisional government was to call elections to a constitutional assembly. Getúlio Vargas was already a well-established politician during the old republic, before he became the main civilian leader of the 1930 Revolution: he had been governor of Rio Grande do Sul, a deputy, a minister, and was a presidential candidate in 1930 election, standing against the nominated candidate of president Washington Luis.[2] If we can trace his ideological origins, the most important influence was probably the authoritarian positivism of Julio de Castilhos, the all-powerful governor of his native state, Rio Grande do Sul, in the turn of the century.[3] With its vague authoritarian and anti-oligarchic party programme, after taking power Vargas's provisional government was in no rush to establish a new constitutional order, and instead almost immediately set about strengthening central power through the appointment of trusted *interventores* in each of the states. However, the Constitutionalist Revolt of 1932, an insurrection led by the State of São Paulo that demanded the restoration of the 1898 liberal Constitution and which was defeated by Vargas, caused him to call a constitutional assembly to approve a new Constitution in 1934.

With an army strengthened by the conflict, he accepted the elections but had strong reservations about the new Constitution that limited his power and restricted his mandate to just one term. From 1934 to 1937, a number of crises were marked by political polarization and tensions that suggested either the reestablishment of the liberal order or a strengthening of authoritarianism with the growing importance of two extra-parliamentary radical political movements: the fascists of AIB and the communist-supported National Liberation Alliance (ANL – Aliança Nacional Libertadora).

Following an attempted putsch led by ANL in November 1935, Vargas declared a state of siege and 'war on communism', reinforcing his alliance with the military leadership and civilian conservatives forces, including the Catholic Church. The repressive apparatus was dramatically extended, with the banning, arrest, and purge of left-wing activists. When, after several extensions of the state of emergency, the majority in Congress called for it to end and, faced with his inability to stand for re-election in 1938 and after some hesitations, Vargas and his associates decided to act. Inventing a fake communist conspiracy, the 'Cohen Plan', and with the support of the head of the army, Vargas decreed the New State dictatorship on 10 November 1937.[4]

Corporatism peaked with the New State, but its ideological and institutional presence had been a part of the official political discourse since 1930. At the start of 1931, Vargas was clear when he declared that one of his goals was to 'destroy the political oligarchs and to establish representation by class rather than through the old system of individual representation that was flawed as an expression of the popular will'.[5] The adoption of corporatism was, therefore, a trademark of the 1930 Revolution that immediately shaped both the elections to the constitutional assembly and the 1934 Constitution.[6] Throughout the 1930s, corporatism – which was associated with authoritarianism, centralism, and nationalism – was assumed by several different emerging political forces, ranging from fascists to social Catholics and 'passing through several *tenentista* and Getulista factions'. The political discourse in favour of technical governments was also very powerful during this period.

Around 40 deputies to the 1933 constitutional assembly represented professional interests, and debates between the different options for corporatist representation were intense. With the 1934 Constitution, corporatist representation became a fact at both federal and the regional level. The cleavage between the liberals and corporatists, and within this latter group was clear. The most polarizing aspect of the debate concerned the powers of the corporatist institutions (about whether they were to be consultative or deliberative) and whether representation would be through technical councils or in parliament. This latter option was chosen, with Vargas's support, for the constitutional assembly, against the proposals that were supported by business groups in the Federation of Industries of the State of São Paulo (FIESP – Federação das Indústrias do Estado de São Paulo).[7] Integral corporatist representation of the type proposed by the AIB was always a minority view. While discussing the option for a bicameral parliament, the 1934 Constitution established a mixed parliament, with the same number of professional and direct elected representatives of the previous constitutional assembly.

Social corporatism was implemented with the establishment of the Ministry of Labour, Industry, and Commerce (MTIC – Ministério do Trabalho, Indústria e Comércio) in 1930, which was also known as the 'ministry of revolution'.[8] The eminent corporatist intellectual Oliveira Viana was appointed legal adviser to the MTIC in 1932. Decree 19.700 of March 1931 gradually replaced independent trade unions with state-controlled syndicates. At the same time several measures, including the eight-hour day, paid holidays and many other benefits were progressively introduced. The 1934 Constitution restored some trade union independence; however, with the declaration of the state of emergency in 1935, they were once more subjected to the state's corporatist intervention, later fully institutionalized.

AIB was perhaps the most important fascist movement in Latin America, and like its European counterparts made corporatism part of its political identity and plans for its future integral state.[9] Founded in 1932 by Plínio Salgado, a politician and Catholic and modernist intellectual, its main leaders included Miguel Reale and Gustavo Barroso. AIB quickly grew into a national organization and adopted the militia structure typical of fascist parties.[10] Integral corporatism was supported by many of the movement's founders, including Olbiano de Melo and others, even before they joined the AIB.[11]

AIB's charismatic leader was influenced more by the Portuguese Integralism of António Sardinha (Integralismo Lusitano) and by Charles Maurras than he was by the Italian Fascism. Nevertheless, the AIB's leadership was well aware of European versions of corporatism and its theorists, especially as promoted in Italy and Portugal.[12] Miguel Reale, the AIB's national secretary for doctrine, was influenced more by Italian Fascism, even though he was less enthusiastic with its organic totality.[13] The same could be said of Plínio Salgado, although this element of AIB's political programme was developed largely by Reale, who was the AIB's most structured corporatist ideologue. Reale's model was for a political representation project with the corporations the official bodies in which members of the different professions would be represented. Each corporation would elect its representative to a national corporatist chamber, which, with the Senate to which members of 'non-economic' (i.e. social and cultural) corporations would be sent, would form the bicameral National Congress.[14]

Corporatism was an integral part of the AIB's identity and of the association its leaders and followers made with European fascism. Plínio called for a basic form of corporatism that was created through the organization of professions from the municipal to the national level and which rejected state corporatism.[15] Some years later, the Integralist leader said he wanted to place himself in the centre, midway between Reale's fascism and Jeová Motta's leftist social corporatism.[16] Motta, who came from the Cearense Labour Legion (LCT – Legião Cearense do Trabalho) and who, as a deputy and leader of the AIB's Corporatist Trade Union Service (SSC – Serviço Sindical Corporativo), was an active defender of social corporatism and of the integration of workers into the organization.

When Getúlio Vargas led the 1937 coup, he was supported by the AIB, while Francisco Campos – the minister closest to fascism – was an apparent intermediary; however, the AIB very quickly realized the new regime was not going to give them the political space and integration they desired. Although all other parties were banned, while the AIB was allowed to continue as a think-tank, tensions with the government increased, leading – as in many other cases – to it also being banned and some of its leaders, including Plínio Salgado, exiled, even as many others joined the new regime. Following the AIB's attack on the Guanabara Palace in May 1938, they were persecuted by the New State.

Two intellectual-politicians and close associates of Vargas, Francisco Campos and Oliveira Viana, played decisive roles in the institutionalization of corporatism during the 1930s. While he never held political office, we could add to the list Manoilesco's Brazilian translator, Azevedo Amaral.[17] These three were always present when referring to the relationship between authoritarian intellectuals and Vargas's New State.[18] Their influences were different, however. Campos was undoubtedly Vargas's main ideologist in the late 1930s, as well as serving as minister for education and justice. He wrote the 1937 Constitution and many of Vargas's main proclamations during the early days of the New State. Oliveira Vianna had occupied a senior role within the Ministry of Labour since 1932 and was one of the main authors of the corporatist labour legislation. Azevedo Amaral remained an important publicist and author who was associated with the regime's propaganda apparatus, although he never held formal political office.[19]

Francisco Campos was perhaps the New State's most articulate ideological creator, since it was he who designed the new regime's institutions in the 1937 Constitution, that brought an end to the state of emergency that had existed since 1935.[20] Like Vargas, Campos was more attuned to authoritarian positivism and less influenced in his youth by European Catholic and reactionary traditionalism.[21] Author of a large selection of political theory and law works, Campos began his political career in traditional parties, and following the 1930 Revolution became a fellow traveller with Getúlio Vargas, while at the same time moving towards an elitist anti-parliamentary position. Later he became the main ideologue of the establishment of a personalized dictatorship endowed with propaganda tools and mass organizations.[22] Soon after the 1930 coup, he and Gustavo Capanema organized the government-supported fascist-style militia, the October Legion. He served as minister of education and health in 1931 and in 1937 was appointed minister of justice. Campos was the principal author of Vargas's coup proclamation and stood in the background directing the dictator's authoritarian discourse throughout the regime's early years as the New State was being institutionalized, although many of its principals never got off the paper.[23]

Campos was a great legitimizer of an authoritarian state as the only alternative to the 'anachronism' of liberal democratic institutions in a mass society. He wrote:

> The masses are fascinated by charismatic personalities. This is what is at the heart of political integration. The larger and more active the masses, the more political integration becomes possible

only through the dictatorship of a personal will. Dictatorship is the political regime of the masses. The only natural expression of the will of the masses is the plebiscite: that is to say, of acclamation and appeal before choice.[24]

Campos was also a supporter of social and political corporatism as the main antidote to communism: as justice minister in 1940, he stated that 'Corporatism kills communism, just as capitalism generates communism'.[25] As other intellectual-politicians of the inter-war period, Campos used alternative concepts of democracy to legitimize the regime, but even as he tried to situate his authoritarian projects midway between liberal and totalitarian experiences, Campos stood closer to the latter than to the former. The 'exaltation of the leader, the break with democratic institutions and the dialogue with intellectuals who inspired fascism is very clear', to the extent that even supporters of the New State noticed.[26] As Vargas's secretary was to write: 'Let's acknowledge that the accusation [of fascism] was not a lie'.[27] It was probably this association with fascism that led Vargas to not reappointing Campos in the government when the international winds changed direction in 1942.

Oliveira Viana, one of Brazil's leading intellectuals in the first half of the twentieth century, served as legal adviser to the MTIC from 1932 to 1940.[28] No examination of Brazilian authoritarianism or corporatism can avoid Oliveira Viana, as he was the leading figure in the project of instrumental authoritarianism – that is, presenting an authoritarian regime as the means of overcoming the dilemmas of Brazil's modernization.[29] Viana's modernizing approach was less present other Latin American corporatists: in fact, he 'perceived himself, and was perceived by others, to be a modern, scientific thinker – not a nostalgic reactionary'.[30]

Oliveira Viana's corporatist project was the central element to legitimize the transformation of the state and to be the main bulwark for the social peace that would get the country moving from top to bottom.[31] His 'authoritarian democracy [was a] democracy with authority, and not liberty, as its essential principle' and that it also should not have such political institutions as a single party.[32] 'A sovereign president, who exerts his power in the name of the nation, and is subordinate to and dependent upon it alone', ought to be enough, since parties were the vehicles of the oligarchy: 'the New State is not a single-party regime: it is a single-president regime'.[33]

When he was appointed to the Itamaraty Commission charged with preparing the first draft of the 1934 Constitution, Viana did not vote for direct corporatist representation in parliament. In his view, the corporatist political representation that was popular in European dictatorships could not be implemented in Brazil for the simple reason that corporatist associations were almost non-existent, leading him to argue instead for the establishment of technical councils.[34] Aware that Vargas had banned parties – even although they continued to exist at the municipal level – Viana though it was 'necessary to abolish their component parts', and that there was only one way to achieve this – through the corporatization of municipal representation with the establishment of 'obligatory professional representation in the establishment of municipal councils'.[35]

To emphasize the instrumental and transitory nature of his authoritarianism, Viana differentiated his project from the Italian Fascist model, stressing the technico-juridical nature of his approach and restating both Manoilesco and the New Deal jurists, but all the while maintaining the authoritarian model.[36] In fact, while his legislative contribution was largely restricted to social corporatism, as far as Viana was concerned, 'the corporatist project and the strengthening of the presidential system of government were the two touchstones of the new authoritarian democracy'.[37] A president, we must not forget, that Viana wanted to be elected by a corporatist electoral college of political, administrative, professional, and cultural institutions. While as a consultant to the Labour Ministry, he was not the only author of the legislation shaping Brazilian social corporatism, he was its backbone and the leading Brazilian exponent of the 'corporatist utopia of the good society'.[38]

During the 1930s, the Brazilian Catholic Church redoubled its struggle against communism. Ever since the 1930 Revolution, the Church had followed and moved closer to Getúlio Vargas in an apparent 're-encounter with the state'.[39] Catholic corporatism also followed this dynamic, both in the Church's independent activities and through its collaboration with the Ministry of Labour, with which Catholic experts had been involved since 1931 in drawing up corporatist legislation. The press and intellectuals surrounding Catholic Action highlighted European models such as Salazar's New State.[40] Under the leadership of Cardinal Sebastião Leme, who was archbishop of Rio de Janeiro from 1930 to 1942, the programme to 're-Christianize society' was developed as the reapproximation of the Church and state continued during the 1930s. The Constitution of 1934 re-established religious education in public schools, provided public financial support for Catholic organizations and secured a convergence between Catholic social corporatism and the projects being promoted by Vargas.

New State of Getúlio Vargas 75

While officially remaining neutral, layman Catholic intellectuals such as Alceu de Amoroso Lima spoke out in favour of this corporatist convergence during the 1930s, even although Cardinal Leme had not offered explicit support to his proposal for the creation of a Catholic party. The cardinal was considerably sympathetic to the fascist AIB, an organization in which many Catholic laymen, and even priests, held senior political offices. In a confidential statement issued in September 1937, Cardinal Leme stated 'that it [Integralism] presently constitutes one of the social forces best organized to defend God, nation and family against atheistic communism' and that its programme of social reforms 'closely follows the whole orientation of Catholic doctrine'.[41] Leme came out in support of the 1937 Coup, the leaders of which he said 'Providence has entrusted the destiny of Brazil'.[42] He also spoke in favour of its agreements with the New State, silencing voices that disagreed with the state corporatism of Getúlio Vargas, which shared a similar dynamic with other authoritarian experiments of the time.

The Constitution of 1937, which was written by the minister of justice, Francisco Campos, was directly inspired by the Polish Constitution introduced by Pilsudsky in 1935, and which gave the president extensive powers and legislative authority.[43] Legislative power was formally exercised by a parliament elected by an electoral college largely consisting of members of the council of municipalities and the federal council that replaced the Senate, consisting of representatives of the States and ten presidential nominees.

The National Economy Council (CEN – Conselho da Economía Nacional) collaborated with parliament. CEN was a consultative chamber, consisting of five sections (Industry and Crafts, Agriculture, Commerce, Transport, and Credit) and made up of representatives of several branches of national production, that was designed to promote the corporatist organization of the national economy. As a law professor and supporter of Vargas wrote in 1937, in a clear reference to the Portuguese New State Constitution of 1933, 'The CEN will be our Corporate Chamber'.[44] Its members were elected by their respective associations, with 'equal representation for employees and employers'.[45] All legislation affecting the national economy had to be submitted to it for review, which also gave it some legislative authority. Its members were chosen by an electoral college made up of unions and employers organizations. The President of the Republic was also elected by corporatist bodies (local authorities, CEN, chamber of deputies, federal council).

There were extensive principles in the Constitution concerning the corporatist foundations of national production that ensured the economy of national labour would be organized in a corporation.[46] Like other authoritarian constitutions and labour codes of the 1930s, the inspiration of Italian Labour Charter was evident, with Article 135 of the new Constitution reproducing, almost word-for-word, Articles 7 and 9 of the Italian charter.[47] For Getúlio's secretary and most observers at the time, the most obvious aspect of its fascist inspiration was the 'chapter on economic organization based on corporatism'.[48] In the New State Constitution, the break with liberalism was much clearer than in other dictatorships of the fascist era.

Although it wasn't put to a plebiscite or implemented, the 1937 charter was the ideal-type regime reflected in the propaganda.[49] In his speeches, Vargas often spoke about the legitimacy of the new Constitution as the foundation of the New State that had replaced political democracy with economic democracy.[50]

The new Information and Propaganda Department (DIP – Departamento de Informação e Propaganda) that was established in 1939 and which reported directly to the President of the Republic coordinated the creation of Vargas's image as well as the regime's censorship and cultural policy. DIP, which was responsible for the systemization of an ideal-type of state and society relations in the New State, had functions very similar to those of its European peers, ranging from Italian Fascism to Salazar's SPN (Secretariado para a Propaganda Nacional). Just like them, DIP published dozens of texts in which corporatism was presented as the official model for the new regime, both at the elite and mass level.[51]

The word chief also began to be used to define Vargas's leadership, especially during the 1 May celebrations, when Vargas was associated with the new official unions and workers in general.[52] New nationalist civic ceremonies, such as the hour of independence and the youth parade were used to involve youth in the new regime, despite the failure to create the national youth organization Francisco Campos had proposed in 1938.[53] These events, along with the other symbols of proximity to European fascism, did not begin to disappear until after Brazil entered the Second World War on the side of the Allies.[54]

The New State did not create a single or dominant party. Following the AIB putsch of 1938, several New State strategists, including Francisco Campos and his private secretary Luis Vergara, advised Vargas to create a single party, which Vargas then sought to do. A series of meetings were held to discuss creating a regime-supporting party that would be formed around the powerful *interventores* in each of the states. It even had a name: National Civic Legion (LCN – Legião

Cívica Nacional). However, there was also opposition to this proposal from among various members of regional elites, and Vargas feared any new party could create a focus for tensions that could weaken his hold on power.

In many official New State documents, the term 'political' was often replaced by 'administration', praising 'technicians as a counterpoint to politics, which was described as the dirty side of private interests'.[55] In fact, bureaucratic-administrative centralization was a trait of the dictatorship and throughout the New State's eight-year duration Vargas provided continuity both to the restructuring of the Brazilian state from a more interventionist perspective and for economic nationalism. Several important steps were also taken to promote political and administrative centralization under the authoritarian command of the National Chief.

One month after the coup, and with the support of the majority of governors, and despite resistance and compromise, *interventores* became the main actors in the political centralization of state leaderships.[56] *Interventores* had executive and legislative powers at the regional level that transformed them into political coordinators who could 'interlink New State oligarchies, ministers and the President of the Republic'.[57] From April 1939, these *interventores* were made responsible to the administrative departments that replaced elected state assemblies and were granted the power to approve budgets and issue decree laws. The members of these bodies were nominated by the president. Needless to say, the party elites, while weakened, survived and 'negotiated' within these new structures at the regional level, in a process of partial continuity and renewal.[58]

Another important feature of the New State administration was the multiplication and overlapping of different bureaucratic-administrative bodies that allowed the intervention of the federal government. Some of these had been created during the 1930s, such as the technical councils, institutes and other federal agencies that became important instruments of economic planning, coordination, and regulation.[59] In 1938, Vargas established the Public Service Administration Department (DASP – Departamento Administrativo do Serviço Público), a federal institution that reported directly to the president that was granted control over all civil servants in the federal government, charged with creating efficient bureaucrats who identified with the modernizing and authoritarian ethos of the New State. This was another instrument of integration between the federal, state, and municipal levels of administration, against particularisms and party politics. In the absence of a single party and a corporatist or authoritarian parliament, these New State governing bodies replaced the traditional representation channels to become the focus for lobbying and the exertion of political pressure. As a contemporary academic observer remarked, Brazil under Vargas became 'Technically, a (non-party) full-fledged dictatorship'.[60]

As Vargas proclaimed in the 1938 May Day celebration,

> I came to establish harmony and tranquillity between employees and their employers [...] However, harmony and tranquillity between employees and employers is not enough. The collaboration of all in the spontaneous effort and common labours are required for the good of this harmony.[61]

The new regime crowned the victory of social corporatism in an authoritarian setting, and on 1 May 1943, after nearly a decade of social legislation, the Consolidated Labour Laws (CLT), which finally systematized and applied labour legislation in Brazil, were introduced.

In 1939, the trade unions became subordinate to the state, losing their organizational independence. In 1940, Vargas established the minimum wage and in 1941, the labour courts.[62] Union funds were tightly controlled and the *imposto sindical* (the compulsory union tax) was created, the intention of which was to provide health and welfare benefits for union members. Union leaders were vetted by the political police. As in some other corporatist dictatorships, any kind of national confederation of labour was banned. Unions were organized in industry-wide syndicates which had a monopoly of representation within a tripartite system of conciliation and arbitration that was largely modelled on Italian Fascist legislation. State protection came under almost total union control, which was opposed by many employers.[63] Social Catholic organizations feared this statist social corporatism while promoting a more pluralist and societal approach. Industrialists reacted to this statist approach as well, although with Vargas being partially successful with their integration into the new structures of social peace.[64]

One student of the Brazilian labour movement noted that the fascist label 'fails to capture the intellectual and legal origins of the social and labour legislation that preceded 1937'.[65] While the clearly authoritarian and Catholic hand of Oliveira Vianna drafted much of the labour legislation, other contributors had also been present since the early 1930s. In fact, Vianna stood alongside integralists, traditionalist Catholics and 'a widening array of lawyers [who were] drawn into the elaboration, re-elaboration and administration of social and labour legislation'.[66] This was the case of many of the labour codes introduced by authoritarian regimes in Europe and Latin America as well. As the ABC of political analysis notes, similar structures may have very different functions across political systems, and in the case of Vargas's Brazil, corporatism left a legacy of inclusion that 'allowed a claim to citizenship and a legitimate voice in public life'.[67]

From 1942, the New State's authoritarian institutional innovation lost its impetus. The international factor and the US's Pan-American strategy in Latin America also had a big impact on Brazil, so this new dynamic could not have been strange. In the late 1930s, Vargas took a pragmatic stance in his foreign policy, attempting to take advantage of the rivalry between the great powers. After the 1937 coup, this position remained unchanged.[68] In 1938 though, Vargas distanced himself from the native fascism represented by the AIB, repressed Nazi-inspired movements and declared the German ambassador *persona non grata*. Notwithstanding the reservations of some segments of the army leadership, Brazil broke off relations with the Axis and became the first Latin American country to declare war on the Axis powers, and the only one sending troops to the front in Europe.[69] During the war years, Brazil got in turn 70 per cent if all US aid given to Latin America.[70]

In 1943, Vargas began to suggest that there would, eventually, be a move towards democratization just as he, rather ironically, began organizing a top-down party ahead of elections.[71] Vargas's social corporatism sought to create an apolitical labour movement consisting of unions that would function as consultative organs of government, with a model of class harmony and collaboration, but from 1943, when Vargas was anticipating a process of regime change, he started to make a direct appeal to the working class.[72] In 1944, Minister of Labour, Alexandre Macondes Filho, called for a plebiscite that was never carried out, proposing a 'semi-corporatist' state, with a CEN complementing, rather than replacing, the legislature.[73] The regime began to recognize and accept the political and electoral potential of organized labour, and Vargas strengthened his links with the working class, allowing union elections and even tolerating strikes, which, under the labour law, were illegal. *Trabalhismo* and the 'populist' Vargas was in the making.[74] The military, afraid of this dynamic, overthrew Vargas in 1945, but many of the legacies of the Estado Novo survived and even the 'Father of the Poor' would come back in the 1950s.[75]

Notes

1. For an excellent brief introduction to the period in English see L. Bethell, 'Politics in Brazil under Vargas, 1930–1945', in L. Bethell, ed., *The Cambridge History of Latin America*, Cambridge, Cambridge University Press, 2008, pp. 1–86.
2. M. C. D'Araujo, ed., *Getúlio Vargas*, Brasília, Biblioteca Digital da Camara dos Deputados, 2011.
3. J. R. Hentschkke, *Positivismo ao Estilo Gaucho: A Ditadura de Júlio de Castilhos e o seu Impacto sobre a Construção do Estado e da Nação no Brasil de Getúlio Vargas*, Porto Alegre, ediPUCRS, 2015.
4. On the ideological dimensions of this polarization, see E. Dutra, *O Ardil Totalitário: Imaginário no Brasil dos Anos 30*, Rio de Janeiro, Editora da UFRJ, 1997.
5. G. Vargas, *A Nova Política do Brasil*, Rio de Janeiro, J. Olympio, 1938, p. 314.
6. V. A. Cepêda, 'Contexto político e crítica à democracia liberal: A proposta de representação classista na Constituinte de 1934', *Perspectivas*, Volume 35, 2009, pp. 211–42; C. M. R. Viscardi, 'A representação profissional na Constituição de 1934 e as origens do corporativismo no Brasil', in Pinto and Martinho, eds., *A Onda Corporativa*, pp. 199–221.
7. A. A. de B. Barreto, 'Representação das associações profissionais no Brasil: O debate dos anos 30', *Revista de Sociologia Política*, Volume 22, 2004, pp. 119–33.
8. F. C. P. Martinho, 'Elites políticas e intelectuais e o Ministério do Trabalho: 1931/1945', *Estudos Ibero-Americanos*, Volume 42, Number 2, 2016, pp. 454–70.
9. L. P. Gonçalves and O. C. Neto, 'Brazilian integralism and the corporatist intellectual triad', *Portuguese Studies,* Volume 32, Number 2, 2016, pp. 225–43.
10. For a brief introduction in English, see M. Klein, *Our Brazil Will Awake! The Acção Integralista Brasileira and the Failed Quest for a Fascist Order in the 1930s*, Amsterdam, Centre for Latin American Research and Documentation, 2004.
11. O. de Melo, *A República Sindicalista dos Estados Unidos do Brasil*, Rio de Janeiro, Tipografia Sal de Terra, 1931.
12. L. P. Gonçalves, *Plínio Salgado: Um Católico Integralista entre Portugal e o Brasil (1895–1975)*, São Paulo, FGV, 2018. See also M. Reale, *Perspectivas Integralistas*, São Paulo, Odeon, 1935.
13. M. Reale, *O Estado Moderno: (Liberalismo, Fascismo, Integralismo)*, Rio de Janeiro, José Olympio, 1934.
14. J. F. Bertonha, 'The corporatist thought in Miguel Reale: Readings of Italian fascism in Brazilian *integralismo*', *Revista Brasileira de História*, Volume 33, Number 66, 2013, p. 233. See also F. Cazetta, 'Da Grécia Antiga ao estado integral: Propostas políticas e o respaldo histórico construído por Miguel Reale', *Mediações*, Volume 19, Number 1, 2014, pp. 102–18.
15. H. Trindade, *A Tentação Fascista no Brasil: Imaginário de Dirigentes e Militantes Integralistas*, Porto Alegre, UFRG Editora, 2016, p. 115.
16. Ibid.

17 A. de C. Gomes, 'The appropriation of Manoilescu's *The Century of Corporatism* in Vargas' Brazil', in Pinto and Finchelstein, eds., *Authoritarianism and Corporatism*, pp. 218–36. For a comparative study of theories of development and dependency, comparing Manoilescu's Rumania and Brazil, see J. L. Love, *Crafting the Third World: Theorizing Underdevelopment in Rumania and Brazil*, Stanford, CA, Stanford University Press, 1996.
18 On the central importance of intellectuals to the Vargas regime and its cultural policy, see S. Micelli, *Intelectuais e Classe Dirigente no Brasil, 1920–1945*, Rio de Janeiro, Difel, 1979; D. Williams, *Culture Wars in Brazil: The First Vargas Regime*, Durham, NC, Duke University Press, 2001.
19 A. Amaral, *O Estado Autoritário e a Realidade Nacional*, Rio de Janeiro, José Olympio Editora, 1938. See L. L. de Oliveira, 'O pensamento de Azevedo Amaral', in L. L. de Oliveira, M. P. Velloso and Â. M. de Castro Gomes, eds., *Estado Novo: Ideologia e Poder*, Rio de Janeiro, Zahar Editores, 1982, pp. 48–9.
20 R. D. dos Santos, 'Francisco Campos e os fundamentos do constitucionalismo antiliberal no Brasil', *Dados: Revista de Ciências Sociais*, Volume 50, Number 2, 2007, pp. 281–323; 'Ditadura e corporativismo na Constituição de 1937: O projeto centralizador e antiliberal de Francisco Campos', in Pinto and Martinho, eds., *A Onda Corporativa*, pp. 285–306.
21 L. A. Abreu, 'O sentido democrático e corporativo da não-Constituição de 1937', *Estudos Históricos*, Volume 29, Number 58, 2016, pp. 461–80. On Alberto Torres, see M. F. L. Fernandes, 'O pensamento político de Alberto Torres: A reforma constitucional e o estado brasileiro', in G. N. Ferreira and A. Botelho, eds., *Revisão do Pensamento Conservador: Ideias e Política no Brasil*, São Paulo, HUCITEC, 2010, pp. 95–118. For the influence of Torres on Oliveira Vianna, see V. A. Cepêda, 'Trajetórias do corporativismo no Brasil: Teoria social, problemas económicos e efeitos políticos', in L. A. de Abreu and P. B. Santos, eds., *A Era do Corporativismo: Regimes, Representações e Debates no Brasil e em Portugal*, Porto Alegre, EdiPUCRS, 2017, pp. 99–149.
22 F. Campos, *O Estado Nacional e as suas Diretrizes*, Rio de Janeiro, Imprensa Nacional, 1937. On Campos's and Oliveira Viana's anti-parliamentarism, see R. Bueno, 'A evolução autoritária brasileira pela via da crítica parlamentar em Francisco Campos e Oliveira Viana', *Revista Filosófica de Coimbra*, Volume 50, 2016, pp. 415–44.
23 M. A. C. dos Santos, 'Francisco Campos: Um ideólogo para o Estado Novo', *Locus: Revista de História*, Volume 13, Number 2, 2007, pp. 31–48.
24 F. Campos, *O Estado Nacional: Sua Estructura, Seu Conteúdo Ideológico*, Rio de Janeiro, José Olympio, 1940, p. 16.
25 Cit. in J. D. French, *Drowning in Laws: Labor Law and Brazilian Political Culture*, Chapel Hill, University of North Carolina Press, 2004, p. 15. See F. Campos, *Direito Constitucional*, Rio de Janeiro, Forense, 1942, pp. 315–16.
26 C. Viscardi, 'The authoritarian wave in the interwar in Brazil: Francisco Campos and his European intellectual networks', unpublished paper, 2017.
27 L. Vergara, *Fui Secretário de Getúlio*, Rio de Janeiro, Editora Globo, 1960, p. 144.

28 There is an extensive bibliography on Oliveira Viana. In English, see L. A. de Abreu, 'Portuguese origins and the "true" Brazil: The corporative vision of Oliveira Viana', *Portuguese Studies*, Volume 32, Number 2, 2016, pp. 199–224.
29 W. G. dos Santos, *Décadas de Espanto e uma Apologia Democrática*, Rio de Janeiro, Rocco, 1998, p. 3.
30 J. D. Needell, 'History, race, and the state in the thought of Oliveira Viana', *The Hispanic American Historical Review*, Volume 75, Number 1, 1995, p. 28.
31 E. Vieira, *Autoritarismo e Corporativismo no Brasil*, São Paulo, Cortez, 1981, p. 133.
32 O. Viana, *O Idealismo da Constituição*, São Paulo, Editora Nacional, 1939, p. 149.
33 Ibid., pp. 210, 149. See R. D. dos Santos, 'Oliveira Vianna e o constitucionalismo no Estado Novo: Corporativismo e representação política', *Sequência*, Number 61, 2010, pp. 273–307.
34 Viana, *O Idealismo da Constituição*, pp. 260–7.
35 Ibid., p. 197.
36 F. Gentile, 'Fascism and corporatism in the thought of Oliveira Vianna: A creative appropriation', in Pinto and Finchelstein, eds., *Authoritarianism and Corporatism in Europe and Latin America*, pp. 180–99. For a version of how Oliveira Vianna defended corporatism in Brazil by emphasising its parallels with the US New Deal, see M. Teixeira, 'Making a Brazilian New Deal: Oliveira Vianna and the transnational sources of Brazil's corporatist experiment', *Journal of Latin American Studies*, Volume 50, Number 3, 2018, pp. 613–41.
37 Â. de C. Gomes, 'Autoritarismo e corporativismo no Brasil: O legado de Vargas', *Revista USP*, Number 65, 2005, p. 113.
38 Ibid.
39 de Sousa, *Círculos Operários*, p. 135.
40 Sousa, *Círculos Operários*, pp. 179, 181.
41 Cit. in M. T. Williams, 'Church and state in Vargas's Brazil: The politics of cooperation', *Journal of Church and State*, Volume 18, Number 3, 976, p. 452.
42 Cit. in Williams, Ibid., p. 457.
43 *Constituição dos Estados Unidos do Brasil*, Rio de Janeiro, Imprensa Nacional, 1937.
44 Cit. in M. Teixeira, 'Law and legal networks in the interwar corporatist turn: The case of Brazil and Portugal', in Pinto and Finchelstein, eds., *Authoritarianism and Corporatism in Europe and Latin America*, p. 208.
45 Ibid., p. 10.
46 Ibid., p. 8.
47 See a comparative table with the *Labour Charter* in French, *Drowning in Laws*, p. 18.
48 Vergara, *Fui Secretário de Getúlio*, p. 144.
49 The pioneering (if sympathetic) book of the German political scientist Karl Loewenstein is still a very interesting study of the political system of Vargas' New State. See his *Brazil under Vargas*, New York, NY, Macmillan, 1942.
50 See his speeches of 1940 in M. C. D'Araujo, ed., *Getúlio Vargas*, Brasília, Câmara dos Deputados, 2011, p. 399.

51 See, for example, the DIP publication *Cultura*, at the elite level. Adriano Nervo Codato and Walter Guandalini Ir, 'Os autores e suas idéias: Um estudo sobre a elite intelectual e o discurso político do Estado Novo', *Estudos Historicos*, Number 32, 2003, p. 152. For one of many exemples at the mass level see, A. F. de Almeida, *A Constituição de 10 de Novembro: Explicada ao Povo*, Rio de Janeiro, DIP, 1940.
52 See, for example, *Da Independência ao Estado Novo*, Rio de Janeiro, DIP, undated. See also A. Paranhos, *O Roubo da Fala: Origens da Ideologia do Trabalhismo no Brasil*, São Paulo, Boitempo, 1999.
53 The proposal by Francisco Campos, clearly inspired in the European models, were opposed by the minister of war and Capanema. In 1939, a more moderate version was finally created: the Brazilian Youth. However, this organization did not develop and it was abolished in 1944. See J. S. B. Horta, *O Hino, o Sermão e a Ordem do Dia: A Educação no Brasil (1930–1945)*, Rio de Janeiro, Editora UFRJ, 1994, p. 64; S. Schwartzman, H. M. B. Bomeny and V. M. R. Costa, eds., *Tempo de Capanema*, Rio de janeiro, Paz e Terra-FGV, 2000, pp. 139–56; M. Parada, *Educando Corpos e Criando a Nação: Cerimónias Civícas e Práticas Disciplinares no Estado Novo*, Rio de Janeiro, Apicuri-PUCRio, 2009.
54 S. Schwartzman, ed., *Estado Novo, um Auto-Retrato: O Arquivo Gustavo Capanema*, Brasília, Editora da Universidade de Brasília, 1983, p. 5.
55 M. C. D'Araujo, *O Estado Novo*, Rio de Janeiro, Zahar, 2000, p. 31.
56 A. Codato, 'Os mecanismos institucionais da ditadura de 1937: Uma análise das contradições do regime de Interventorias Federais nos estados', *História*, Volume 32, Number 2, 2013, pp. 189–208.
57 S. Goulart, *Sob a Verdade Oficial: Ideologia, Propaganda e Censura no Estado Novo*, São Paulo, Marco Zero, 1990, p. 29.
58 A. Codato, 'Estado Novo no Brasil: Um estudo da dinâmica das elites políticas regionais em contexto autoritário', *DADOS: Revista de Ciências Sociais*, Volume 58, Number 2, 2015, p. 321; L. A. de Abreu, *Um Olhar Regional sobre o Estado Novo*, Porto Alegre, EdPUCRGS, 2007.
59 C. A. A. Albernaz, 'The technical councils of the Brazilian government structure: Corporatism, authoritarianism and modernization (1934–1945)', *Portuguese Studies*, Volume 32, Number 2, 2016, pp. 244–61.
60 Loewnstein, *Brazil under Vargas*, p. 370.
61 D'Araújo, *Getúlio Vargas*, p. 375.
62 F. T. da Silva, 'The Brazilian and Italian labor courts: Comparative notes', *International Review of Social History*, Number 55, 2010, pp. 381–412. For an analysis of the more diverse inspiration of the creation of the Brazilian labour courts, see A. de C. Gomes and F. T. da Silva, 'Labor Courts in Brazil: Their origins, challenges and expansion', in L. Fink and J. Palacio, eds., *Labor Justice across the Americas*, Urbana, University of Illinois Press, pp. 211–34.
63 I. Roxborough, 'Urban labour movements in Latin America since 1930', in L. Bethell, ed., *Latin America: Politics and Society since 1930*, Cambridge, Cambridge University Press. 1998, p. 232.
64 B. Weinstein, *For Social Peace in Brazil: Industrialists and the Remaking of Working Class in São Paulo, 1920–1964,* Chapel Hill, University of North Carolina Press, 1996.
65 French, *Drowning in Laws*, p. 16.

66 Ibid., p. 21.
67 B. Weinstein, 'Post-colonial Brazil', in J. C. Moya, ed., *The Oxford Handbook of Latin American History*, Oxford, Oxford University Press, 2011, p. 234.
68 B. Fausto, *Concise History of Brazil*, Cambridge, Cambridge University Press, 1999, pp. 222–3.
69 L. Bethell, 'Politics in Brazil under Vargas, 1930–1945', in L. Bethell, ed., *The Cambridge History of Latin America*, p. 67.
70 R. M. Levine, *Father of the Poor? Vargas and His Era*, Cambridge, Cambridge University Press, 1998, p. 71.
71 J. D. French, 'The populist gamble of Getúlio Vargas in 1945: Political and ideological transitions in Brazil', in D. Rock, ed., *Latin America in the 1940s*, Berkeley, University of California Press, pp. 141–65.
72 Cit. in Collier and Collier, *Shaping the Political Arena*, p. 173.
73 M. Teixeira, 'Law and legal networks in the interwar corporatist turn', in Pinto and Finchelstein, eds, *Authoritarianism and Corporatism in Europe and Latin America*, p. 209.
74 See especially Â. de C. Gomes, *A Invenção do Trabalhismo*, Rio de Janeiro, FGV Editora, 2005, and J. Ferreira, *Trabalhadores do Brasil: O Imaginario Popular (1930–1945)*, Rio de Janeiro, FGV, 1997; J. Ferreira, ed., *O Populismo e a sua História: Debate e Crítica*, Rio de Janeiro, Civilização Brasileira, 2001.
75 J. M. de Carvalho, 'Vargas e os militares', in D. Pandolfi, eds., *Repensar o Estado Novo*, Rio de Janeiro, FGV, pp. 342–4; L. O. Silva, 'A "política do exército" no primeiro governo Vargas: 1930–1945', in P. P. Z. Bastos and P. C. D. Fonseca, eds., *A Era Vargas: Desenvolvimentismo, Economia e Sociedade*, São Paulo, UNESP, 2011, pp. 323–79.

11 Lázaro Cárdenas and the permutations of corporatism in authoritarian Mexico

The Mexico of Lázaro Cárdenas had a very paradigmatic relation with the corporatist wave of the 1930s. Elected President of the country in 1934, Cárdenas established a new relationship between the political system and the state and between labour and organized interests, while reorganizing the dominant party, the Party of the Mexican Revolution (PRM– Partido de la Revolución Mexicana) along corporatist lines.[1] Cárdenas's presidency (1934–40) was the true consolidator of the post-revolutionary regime in Mexico – a regime based on presidentialism, the corporatist party, and nationalism.[2] It led to a singular authoritarian corporatist experience associated with the dominant party and, given the secularist cleavage, it re-emerged several times after the revolution with a conservative and radical right-wing opposition counteracting with corporatism of Catholic origin.

The nature of the Cárdenas reforms consolidated a political regime that was difficult for its contemporaries to characterize.[3] As J. H. Plenn wrote in 1939, 'Cardenism is not communism, nor is it Nazism nor fascism, nor "pure" democracy. Yet, it has certain aspects of all four, with the modifications of its own traditions and environment'.[4] The perception of Cárdenas during the 1930s, both in Mexico in particular and Latin America in general, was that he was associated with progressive social and economic policy, secularism, and with the left of the political spectrum, which was also apparent in how he was viewed internationally.[5] Nationalism, secularism, and developmentalism associated with the left marked this view, with a clear separation from the conservative, Catholic, and fascist right.[6]

As another contemporary observer wrote,

> The formula of the Mexican Revolution is *intervention* of the state in economic production as an *element* of control, supervision and

balance and the formation of the government with participation of *all social classes* in a functional, democratic system, or, that is to say, the organization of all sectors of production.[7]

As Cárdenas himself claimed, the Mexican Revolution imposed social democracy (democracia social).[8] Cardenism, therefore, 'represented the last, great reforming phase of the Mexican Revolution',[9] and its legacy consolidated the main characteristics of the Mexican political system: authoritarian, hyper-presidential, corporatist, and nationalist. With the creation of the PRI in 1929, while maintaining some small satellite parties, it became a dominant-party regime, one based more on co-optation than open repression. It became a *dictablanda* or an authoritarian regime 'with pretty features': It was a civilian regime that held regular elections, enjoyed revolutionary legitimacy, and co-opted the country's main interest groups.[10]

The major developments associated with Cárdenas' presidency were agrarian reform, nationalization of the oil industry, the socialist reform of education, the reorganization of trade unions, and the PRM. As one of Mexico's leading historians noted, 'ideological Cárdenas supporters identified with the administration's labour and agrarian reforms, its economic nationalism, socialist education and progressive foreign policy; but they linked these innovative policies to older political traditions of liberal-patriotism, freemasonry and Jacobinism'.[11] The Mexican Constitution of 1917 and the Federal Labour Law of 1931 gave Cárdenas added legitimacy. Not only did the Constitution define a wide range of social rights, but it also foreshadowed active state intervention to achieve its redistributive goals. Cárdenas and the PNR continuously insisted they were merely carrying out the ideas contained in these two documents.

For Cárdenas, the primary function of the modern state was to be an arbiter of the conflicts between capital and labour, lending its support to the working class.[12] The mobilization of labour was bound up with economic nationalism, and Cárdenas soon expressed his strategy towards the labour movement. As far as Cárdenas was concerned, 'Politics and economics must be one and the same thing'. In his famous Monterrey speech of February 1936, he called on the workers to organize themselves into a united front in order to defend their interests more effectively; however, at the same time he also said, 'the employer classes have the same rights as the workers to establish their organizations in a national structure'. This meant that the government would be 'the arbiter and regulator of social life'.[13] The Department of Labour became an agency for working-class organization with Cárdenas calling for a Congress to unify the labour movement, which resulted in the formation of the Confederation of Mexican Workers (CTM – Confederación de Trabajadores Mexicanos). Under the charismatic leadership of Vicente Lombardo Toledano, the CTM became the main instrument for the integration and subordination of the union movement to the state, establishing itself as a united front in a nationalist and anti-fascist 'popular front' environment. This move was also supported by the recently legalized Mexican Communist Party (PCM – Partido Comunista de México).

The creation of a powerful trade union bureaucracy at the service of a labour law that practised almost obligatory arbitration and limited the number of strikes was being consolidated. As Toledano noted in 1940, 'the federal government intervened in almost all important labour disputes'.[14] While the creation of national confederations of peasants and workers was a fact at that same time, the intention to create a national association of employers under the control of the National Economy Secretary was resisted by the employers' confederations. In fact, as several of his Marxist critics pointed out, while his discourse was left-wing, Cárdenas transformed the disorderly Mexican trade union movement into one that was 'regulated and manipulated at the service of a state concerned with improving production in order to boost the development of capitalism'.[15] However, in addition to capitalism, these Marxist critics may have subscribed to the political functions Cárdenas described, although the Single Labour Front projects that were initially announced in his electoral campaign did not necessarily suggest the corporatist reorganization of the PRI.[16] In fact, the reasons that led Cárdenas to push for the corporatization of the party first, in particularly its insertion into the state, were not evident while some more conjunctural factors were also important.

The PNR was the dominant party when Cárdenas was elected president. It had been created by former President Elías Calles in 1929 as a way to unite the dominant factions of the Mexican Revolution.[17] In its formative years, the PNR was little more than a collection of political parties that were gradually subsumed under the central authority of the PNR. This situation changed at the second national convention in Querétaro in December 1933. At that meeting, the nomination of the presidential candidate for the 1934 elections and the elaboration of a political programme for the next government, the so-called Sexenal Plan, was discussed. It also sought to change the party structure to strengthen it with the dissolution of the parties affiliated to it, but without being openly hostile to liberal democracy.

Since at least 1935, Cárdenas had made several calls for the incorporation of organized interests, especially labour unions and peasant organizations, into the PNR, but the formal plans for a new party did not begin until December 1937 and were accelerated as a result of the conflict with Calles. Union organizations had previously resisted maintaining ties with the official party, although Cárdenas, who had briefly served as PNR president in 1930 had made the effort. In 1938, Cárdenas called a national Constituent Congress to reorganize the party, which was then renamed the Party of Mexican Revolution (PRM – Partido de la Revolución Mexicana). Members were invited to this Congress along functional lines representing four sections: workers, peasants, military, and others. This last group included PNR members who did not fit into any other groups: women, young people, professionals, merchants, and workers who did not belong to the workers' federations included in the first section. These sections were brought into the party, giving it an undeniably 'unique internal structure' (Table 11.1).[18]

Cárdenas was to transform this party into a political tool at the service of the president, giving him a structure upon which he could establish solid and lasting dominion over the authoritarian Mexican political system. The main innovation of this reorganization was to give the party its corporatist shape.

The CTM officially affiliated to the PRM with all workers joining the CTM automatically becoming members of the PRM. Trade unions were also invited to join the PRM in such a way that the labour movement's support of the regime became automatic and almost compulsory. While the union movement retained its independence in relation to social bargaining, in the political and electoral fields, it was permitted to operate only within the PRM and to adhere strictly to the regulations issued by the party's leadership.[19]

Table 11.1 The Four Sections of the *Partido de la Revolución Mexicana* (PRM)

Labour	Agrarian	Popular	Military
• Central Labour Organization: CROM, CTM, CGT • National Unions • State, Regional and Municipal Labour Federations	• Central Peasant Organization: CNC • Agrarian Leagues • Peasant Cooperatives	Associations: students, professionals, artisans, tenants, others	Armed forces

Business organizations were excluded from the PRM. Neither the Chamber of Commerce (CONCANACO – Confederación de Cámaras Nacionales de Comercio, Servicios y Turismo) nor the Chamber of Industry (CONCAMIM – Confederación de Cámaras Industriales) was part of the party, although in 1936 Cárdenas introduced the Chambers of Commerce and Industry Law, which brought them together in a single federation and stipulated mandatory membership for companies with capital exceeding the minimum amount allowed by law. In this way, a semi-official institution was created with some capacity of state supervision.

In the end, the PRM reduced the army's political influence, enhanced the centralization of power, and channelled interest organizations by 'confining their revolutionary dynamics into an institutional framework'.[20] The PMR's four sections remained compartmentalized, each with its area, associated in specific organizations. While the CTM did not enjoy an organizational monopoly, it began competing for the nomination of congressional candidates and other party nominations.[21] 'For the first time in history, working-class Mexicans accounted for nearly half the national political leadership'.[22]

Cárdenas's succession was to represent the first test for the new corporatist PMR, when he supported the moderate Ávila Camacho, imposing him on the party while an important segment of the CTM supported a left-wing candidate. With the support of Toledano, the official candidate was eventually endorsed by the CTM, and in the 1940s this alliance was to come to represent the CTM's growing subordination to the state and the ruling party.

Most scholars of Cárdenas claim the source of his inspiration was the example of the Popular Front in Spain and France, which is how he decided to recast the PNR.[23] The declaration of principles and the action programme adopted by the PRM stated its most important task was to prepare the people for the establishment of a workers' democracy as a step towards socialism. Moderate socialism as described by Cárdenas, who said

> Our government [...] is democratic and liberal, with a few moderate traces of socialism that affect land ownership, principally for restitution and in the laws that refer to the relationship between capital and labour, but which are not nearly as radical as those in other democratic countries.[24]

A sort of popular front, 'with overtones of the corporate state of Italy of the 1930s'?[25] Clearly, the right-wing opposition saw nothing of this latter element in Cárdenas's reforms.[26]

Cárdenas's presidency radicalized the 'revolution/counter-revolution' cleavages of the 1930s while opening others among the power elite and within the social field, with even greater polarization between the left and the right. With the creation of the PRM, divisions between business interest groups and segments of the social elites added to the political polarization. However, the conservative and radical right-wing opposition remained relatively powerless to challenge Cardenism, despite having some mobilizing capacity.

The number of opposition parties close to liberal democracy and other parties that had worked with the ruling elite and which were closed to the liberal matrix since the 1920s grew, as did the number of more secular radical right-wing parties; however, it was those movements that were in one way or another associated with the Catholic reaction that was the most important in terms of political mobilization.[27]

The secular cleavage, which periodically re-emerged in Jacobinism versus clericalism conflicts, was behind the most important conservative and radical right-wing organizations that were often associated with segments of the economic and social elite. Most of these developed an authoritarian, anti-Marxist, and anti-parliamentary ultra-nationalism that almost always contained aspects of traditionalist Catholicism.[28] Many of these movements acquired a popular base in earlier violent revolts, such as the Catholic Cristiada. Others, such as Mexican Revolutionary Action (ARM – Acción Revolucionaria Mexicanista) and the Camisas Doradas (Gold Shirts) – an anti-communist nationalist group that was repressed and dissolved by Cárdenas – had more militarized organizations and used symbols that approached those of fascism, to which were joined a number of smaller groups.[29] The most important of these, however, were those closest to Catholicism, including the National Synarchist Union (UNS – Unión Nacional Sinarquista).

Right-wing opposition to Cárdenas was also influenced by the political culture of fascism, particularly Italian Fascism and the reactionary *hispanismo* associated with the dictatorship of Primo de Rivera and the Francoists in the Spanish Civil War.[30] At critical moments, such as the industrial disputes of 1936, the rebellion in 1938 and the electoral dynamics of 1939–40, the term 'fascism' was used to describe several of the radical right-wing groups that were openly hostile to Cárdenas.[31] Several political movements developed among businessmen frightened by Cárdenas social corporatism, which favoured the unions and the left, and within a Catholic Church that was openly hostile to the socialist reform of education.³² One such group was the Middle-Class Confederation (CCM – Confederación de las Clases Medias), which stood close to some employers and intended to unify the entire middle class to counter the current communist tendency associated with Cárdenas. What alternative did the mostly Hispanophile radical-right propose as antidote to the Mexico of Cárdenas? With some variations, it expressed a model that held in common to the organic options of the Catholic-traditionalist corporatism found in most of their European and Latin American contemporaries. In fact, the construction of an anti-individualist organic social model, the central ideas of which were representation 'via intermediate bodies (church, family, university, professional groups, unions, municipalities)' was dominant.³³ This reinforced the difference between the organicist model and official corporatism since while the post-revolutionary state sought to 'organize society in a vertical and coercive way, the conservatives appealed to the medieval model [...] allowing limits to state power, stopping the progress of liberal individualism and harmonizing the economic interests of workers and owners'.³⁴

To these reactionary Hispanicists, their alternative to Cardenism involved anti-liberal organicism and proposed a corporatism that enhanced limits to state intervention. A striking example of this discourse was that of such intellectual-Politician as Salvador Abascal Infante, leader of successive traditionalist, legal and clandestine Catholic movements, including BASE, the Legion, and the UNS.³⁵ Another example was Manuel Gómez Morín, founder of the National Action Party (PAN – Partido de Acción Nacional) in 1939, who had a more modernizing and less clerical outlook.³⁶

Corporatist Catholicism in Mexico developed in a manner similar to that in many Latin American countries and was eventually radicalized by the anti-clerical and secularizing component of the Mexican regime, although with tensions and reconciliations. As highlighted in various contexts,

> *Rerum Novarum* was also a source of inspiration for non-religious movements that shared the hostility to liberalism and socialism, and that saw in the notion of "organic democracy" or in the proposal of the corporate organization of society, useful elements for the integration of an authoritarian model.³⁷

The development of social Catholicism and of Catholic Action in Mexico was much more conditioned than in other Latin American countries. After the emergence of Catholic Action in 1929, the Catholic Church severed its links with society and labour through the creation of the Catholic Labour Confederation (CCT – Confederación Católica del Trabajo). Founded in the 1920s, CCT was virulently anti-communist and was more popular with the middle classes than it was with the working class. The Federal Labour Law of 1931 denied legal recognition to confessional unions, and social Catholicism's activities were severely restricted.[38]

The primacy of more radical organizations associated with political Catholicism became more evident during the 1930s. The National League for the Defence of Freedom of Religion (Liga Nacional de la Defensa de la Libertad de la Religión), for example, expressed a clearly integralist, ultramontane nationalism that was profoundly influenced by the project for a 'Catholic, hierarchical and corporatist society'.[39] Founded by a former League member, the clandestine Legions, which were supported by radical factions within the clergy who were later moderated, based its programme on an electoral system established on 'corporatist plebiscites'.[40] The same could also be said of the more secretive BASE (1934–37), which called for the establishment of a corporatist Christian order in Mexico that was behind the creation of the more powerful UNS in 1937. With powerful support from sections of the Catholic hierarchy and with a more peaceful political mobilization strategy, the UNS, with its paramilitary parades of its Green Shirts and its internal authoritarian structure, acquired a character that was close to fascism.[41] Its political programme was not very different from its predecessors, expressing a view that was more anti-state intervention, anti-socialist – especially in education – and anti-democratic, reinforcing the organic and corporatist model. Basically, 'synarchism became the main representative of a conservative, traditionalist, Hispanicist, nationalist and Catholic society, that did not find a place in the new order of life that post-revolutionary modernity was imposing'.[42] The UNS had peasant support, which led to it becoming a mass organization. Salvador Abascal, UNS leader from 1940, gave the UNR a look that was more Fascist-Falangist, with its hierarchical-militarized organization and its hint of leadership cult.[43]

Initially sharing some of the same ideological references, while recruiting from among the less religious urban middle class, was PAN, which was founded in 1939 under the leadership of Manuel Gómez Morín and Efraín González Luna, with support from lay Catholics and financial backing from some of the interest groups that opposed Cardenism. While its militant base included many who had come up through the Catholic associations, unlike the UNS, PAN did not present itself as a confessional party and distanced itself from the symbolic radicality of the UNS.[44]

Nonetheless, as noted above, the most important group of PAN's founders was that of conservative Catholic activists and Hispanists, while some technocrats that had been associated with the banking and industrial elite were also part of the founding matrix, attracted as they were by its organic model, defence of private ownership and rejection of nationalizations. Morín was quite clearly influenced by and an admirer of the dictatorship of Primo de Rivera in Spain, which struck him as the model of modernizing authoritarianism to follow, particularly the idea of the corporatist state represented by a National Assembly composed of trade unions, the Church, employers' associations and the universities.[45] It was this more modernizing corporatism of Primo de Rivera that Gómez Morín held up in contrast with the official corporatism of Cárdenas.[46] Morín had a much clearer idea of what a political party was and of the functions of government and administration of the country than Luna, who had been a product of social Catholicism and the Catholic CCT union.

PAN's political programme had more in common with the right-wing corporatism found in European and Latin American political culture, and it accused Cárdenas of 'preserving the constitutional liberalism of the Mexican state by making only the party corporatist, while original members of PAN wanted the entire Mexican state to be corporatist'.[47] PAN's political programme clearly represented the other pole of a third way between liberalism and socialism, culminating in a project in which Morín's modernizing authoritarianism united with Luna's more Catholic matrix.[48] PAN's Minimum Political Action Programme distanced itself from the principle of liberal democracy, proposing instead corporatist representation in which the Chamber of Representatives would be occupied by 'the intermediate communities and the economic, social and cultural interests of the nation'.[49] In 1945, its newspaper, *La Nación*, called for 'organic and Catholic democracy', with Luna referring to the regimes of Franco in Spain and Salazar in Portugal.[50]

Following this overview of the nature of the opposition to Cardenism, we can say that 'to a certain extent, radical demands, whether from the left or right, strengthened the establishment of a corporatism system during the Cárdenas era'.[51] However, what is clear is that the dominant pattern of corporatist proposals in Latin America and Europe remained in opposition here, while 'Mihail Manoilescu would not have found the consummation of his corporatist utopia in Cardenism'.[52]

The paradigmatic relationship between Cárdenas and the corporatist wave of the 1930s was due largely to the fact the PRM was probably the first corporatist dominant party, consolidating 'a top-down, monolithic, corporatist, unitary, monopolistic and even authoritarian socio-political structure – while incorporating some liberal, pluralist, participatory and social justice ingredients'.[53]

Notes

1 For an excellent biography of Cárdenas before he became president, see R. Pérez Montfort, *Lázaro Cárdenas: Un Mexicano del Siglo XX*, Vol. 1, México City, Debate, 2018.
2 M. Schettino, *Cien Años de Confusión*, México City, Taurus, 2007, p. 249.
3 For a systematic overview of the interpretations of Mexico's political system up the 1980s, see J. Molinar Horcasitas, 'Escuelas de interpretación del sistema político mexicano', *Revista Mexicana de Sociología*, Volume 55, Number 2, 1993, pp. 3–56.
4 J. H. Plenn, *México Marches*, New York, 1939, pp. 360–1. 'It is quite evident that there are fundamental contradictions in the economic philosophy of the president, some principles bearing a relation at times to fascism and to socialism at others', J. Ashby, 'Labor and the theory of the Mexican Revolution under Lázaro Cárdenas', *The Americas*, Volume 20, Number 2, 1963, p. 194. For Franco Savarino, 'Italian Fascism was an available model and was used discreetly by the various successive governments from Obregón to Cárdenas', while in the 'Messico' entry to the *Enciclopedia Italiana* the PNR is considered identical to the Italian Fascist Party (PNF) and the German Nazi Party (NSDAP), see F. Savarino, 'Los avatares del fascismo en México', in X. P. Campos López and D. M. Velázquez Caballero, eds., *La Derecha Mexicana en el Siglo XX: Agonía, Transformación y Supervivencia,* Puebla, Benemérita Universidad Autónoma de Puebla, 2017, p. 155, and F. Savarino, *México e Italia: Política y Diplomacia en la Época del Fascismo, 1922–1942*, México, SER, 2003.
5 F. E. Schuler, *México between Hitler and Roosevelt: Mexican Foreign Relations in the Age of Lázaro Cárdenas*, Albuquerque, University of New México Press, 1998.
6 See A. M. Kiddle, *México's Relations with Latin America during the Cárdenas Era*, Albuquerque, University of New México Press, 2016.
7 T. Zabre, 'El marxismo en la Revolución MexIcana: Esbozo de una interpretacion historica', *Futuro*, Volume III, 1935, pp. 1–14.
8 *Cárdenas Habla*, México, PRM, 1940, p. 183.
9 A. Knight, 'The end of the Mexican Revolution? From Cárdenas to Ávila Camacho, 1937–1941', in P. Gillingham and B. T. Smith, eds., *Dictablanda: Politics, Work, and Culture in México, 1938–1968*, Durham, NC, Duke University Press, 2014, p. 62.
10 G. Flores-Macías, 'México's PRI: The resilience of an authoritarian successor party and its consequences for democracy', in J. Loxton and S. Mainwaring, eds., *Life after Dictatorship: Authoritarian Successor Parties Worldwide*, Cambridge, Cambridge University Press, 2018, p. 260.

11 A. Knight, 'Cardenismo: Juggernaut or jalopy?', *Journal of Latin American Studies*, Volume 26, Number 1, 1994, p. 80. See also V. Oikión Solano, 'El circulo de poder del Presidente Cárdenas', *Intersticios Sociales*, Volume 3, 2012, pp. 1–36.
12 See J. Ashby, *Organized Labor and the Mexican Revolution under Lázaro Cárdenas*, Chapel Hill, University of North Carolina Press, 1967.
13 L. Cárdenas, *Ideario Político*, México City, Era, 1972, p. 189.
14 Cit. in A. Anguiano, *El Estado y la Política Obrera del Cardenismo*, México City, Era, 1975, p. 130.
15 Ibid., p. 131.
16 I. Semo, 'El cardenismo revisado: La tercera vía y otras utopías inciertas', *Revista Mexicana de Sociología*, Volume 55, Number 2, 1993, p. 221.
17 See L. J. Garrido, *El Partido de la Revolución Institucionalizada (Medio Siglo de Poder Político en México): La Formación del Nuevo Estado (1928–1945)*, Mexico City, Siglo XXI, 1982; A. Córdova, 'La fundación del partido oficial', *Revista Mexicana de Ciencias Políticas y Sociales*, Volume 39, Number 155, 1994, pp. 143–71, and P. Castro Martínez, 'Los partidos de la revolución: Del Partido Liberal Constitucionalista (PLC) a los albores del Partído Nacional Revolucionario (PNR)', *Polis: Investigación y Análisis Sociopolítico y Psicosocial*, Volume 8, 2012, pp. 25–50.
18 K. Park, 'The role of Lázaro Cárdenas in demilitarizing Mexican politics and building the one-party state, 1935–1945', doctoral thesis, University of California Los Angeles, 2000, p. 99.
19 Cit. in T. Maden, *Ideología y Praxis Política de Lázaro Cárdenas*, Mexico City, Siglo XXI, 1972, p. 107.
20 Park, 'The role of Lázaro Cárdenas', p. 114.
21 K. Middlebrook, *The Paradox of Revolution: Labor, the State, and Authoritarianism in Mexico*, Baltimore, MD, Johns Hopkins University Press, 1995, p. 94.
22 See R. A. Camp, *Political Recruitment across Two Centuries: Mexico, 1884–1991*, Austin, University of Texas Press, 1995, p. 176.
23 Park, 'The role of Lázaro Cárdenas', p. 101.
24 Cited in Ashby, 'Labor and the theory of the Mexican Revolution', p. 162.
25 Ibid., p. 161. For a comparative study of the PRI and the PNF, see T. Bertaccini, 'Volver à las orígines del Partido Revolucionario Institucional: Una mirada comparativa com el partido Nacional Fascista', *Revista Electrónica Iberoamericana*, Volume 10, Number 2, 2016, pp. 1–18.
26 For an overview of the right under Cárdenas, see J. W. Sherman, *The Mexican Right: The End of Revolutionary Reform, 1929–1940*, Westport, CT, Praeger, 1997.
27 J. Garciadiego, 'La oposición conservadora y de las classes medias al cardenismo', *Istor: Revista de Historia Internacional*, Volume 7, Number 26, 2006, pp. 30–49.
28 See N. Cárdenas and M. Tenorio, 'México 1920s–1940s: Revolutionary government, reactionary politics', in S. U. Larsen, ed., *Fascism Outside Europe*, New York, NY, SSM-Columbia University Press, 2001, p. 609.
29 A. Gojman de Backal, 'La acción revolucionaria mexicanista y el fascismo en México: Los Dorados', *Jahrbuch für Geschichte Lateinamerikas*, Volume 25, Number 1, 1988, pp. 291–302.

30 R. Montfort, *Por la Patria y por la Raza: La Derecha Secular en el Sexenio de Lázaro Cárdenas*, Mexico City, Universidad Nacional Autónoma de México, 1993.
31 Ibid., p. 10.
32 For a global overview of fascism in Mexico, see Savarino, 'Los avatares del fascismo'.
33 B. Urías Horcasitas, 'Una pasión antirrevolucionaria: El conservadurismo hispanófilo mexicano (1920–1960)', *Revista Mexicana de Sociología*, Volume 72, Number 4, 2010, p. 617.
34 Ibid., pp. 617–8.
35 F. A. García Naranjo, 'Entre la histeria anticomunista y el rencor antiyanqui: Salvador Abascal y los escenarios de la guerra fría en México', *Historia y Memoria*, Volume 10, 2015, pp. 165–98.
36 S. Loaeza, *El Partido Acción Nacional: La Larga Marcha, 1939–1994 – Oposición Leal y Partido de Protesta*, Mexico City, Fondo de Cultura Económica, 1999, and M. T. Gómez Mont, *Manuel Gómez Morín, 1915–1939: La Raíz Simiente de un Proyecto Nacional*, Mexico City, Fondo de Cultura Económica, 2008.
37 S. Loaeza, 'Los orígenes de la propuesta modernizadora de Manuel Gómez Morín', *Historia Mexicana*, Volume XLVI, Number 2, 1996, p. 438.
38 S. J. C. Andes, 'A Catholic alternative to revolution: The survival of social Catholicism in post-revolutionary Mexico', *The Americas*, Volume 68, Number 4, 2012, pp. 529–62.
39 P. Serrano Álvarez, cit. in Cárdenas and Tenorio, 'México 1920s–1940s', p. 615.
40 Cárdenas and Tenório, Ibid., pp. 617–8.
41 There is an extensive bibliography on the relationship between synarchism and fascism. See the pioneering work by J. Meyer, *Le Sinarquisme: Un Fascisme Mexicain? 1937–1947*, Paris, Hachette, 1977. For a critical overview, see B. C. Losfeld, 'No todo lo que brilla es oro: Apuntes sobre la naturaleza del sinarquismo mexicano', *Tzintzun: Revista de Estudios Históricos*, Volume 61, 2015, pp. 130–62.
42 P. Serrano Álvarez, 'El sinarquismo en el bajío mexicano (1934–1951): Historia de un movimiento social regional', *Estudios de Historia Moderna y Contemporánea de México*, Volume 14, 1991, p. 207.
43 Serrano Álvarez, Ibid., p. 216.
44 M. Rodríguez Lapuente, 'El sinarquismo y Acción Nacional: Las afinidades conflictivas', *Foro Internacional*, Volume XXIX, Number 3, 115, 1989, pp. 440–58.
45 Loaeza, 'Los orígenes de la propuesta', pp. 445–7.
46 M. Gómez Morín, *El Régimen Contra la Nación*, Mexico City, Partido Acción Nacional, 1939.
47 H. Gómez Peralta, 'Las raíces anti-sistémicas del Partido Acción Nacional', *Revista Mexicana de Ciencias Políticas y Sociales*, Volume LVII, Number 214, 2012, p. 202, P.-J. Raphaële, 'Modèles et paradoxes de la "contre-révolution" au XXème siècle: Création et évolution du Partido Acción Nacional au Mexique (1939)', *América: Cahiers du CRICCAL*, Volume 33, 2005, p. 69.
48 Loaeza, 'Los orígenes de la propuesta', p. 429.

49 Partido Acción Nacional, *Programa Mínimo de Acción Política*, Mexico, II Convención Nacional del Partido Acción Nacional, 1940, p. 6, cit. in Peralta, 'Las raíces anti-sistémicas', p. 202.
50 E. González Luna, 'Una guerra ideológica: Causas, pretextos, desmanes', *La Nación*, Volume V, Number 212, 3 November 1945, p. 6.
51 Cárdenas and Tenorio, 'México 1920s–1940s', p. 623.
52 I. Semo, 'El cardenismo revisado: La tercera vía y otras utopías inciertas', *Revista Mexicana de Sociología*, Volume 55, Number 2, 1993, pp. 197–223.
53 Wiarda, *Soul of Latin America*, p. 262. For Ilán Semo, the 'statement – extraordinarily disclosed in modern historiography that Cardenismo produced a corporatist order in general is inaccurate' (Semo, 'El cardenismo revisado', p. 22). Middlebrook, for example, does not find it useful because of concept stretching; however, the composition of the party and the state-organized interest relationship 'would merit use of the term corporatism', see Middlebrook, *The Paradox of Revolution*, p. 341.

12 Laureano Gómez and the failure of authoritarian corporatism in Colombia

Laureano Gómez, leader of the Conservative Party (PC – Partido Conservador) from 1933 to 1946, became president of Colombia in 1950 – at time of political polarization and intense inter-party violence. Gómez had been active in Colombian politics since the early 1930s, when he led a fierce opposition to the then governing Liberal Party (PL – Partido Liberal Colombiano). Elected unopposed to the highest political office, he sought to institutionalize an authoritarian and corporatist regime.[1] He was overthrown in 1953, following Colombia's first military coup, led by General Gustavo Rojas Pinilla with the support of leading figures from within the PC and the PL. His ultimately failed attempt to institutionalize an authoritarian regime brought the curtain down on the corporatist wave of the inter-war period.

For most of the first half of the twentieth century, Colombian politics was dominated by two parties – the PC and PL – with regular elections, rotation of government, and which even had a 'record of democratic reforms' during the 1930s.[2] In fact, between 1910 and 1949, despite some periods of political violence and fraud, this oligarchic democracy managed to achieve a reasonable degree of 'political stability, openness and competitiveness'.[3]

The 1930 elections marked the end of the conservative hegemony and the beginning of fifteen years of PL government. It was in the context of opposition to these governments that Laureano Gómez rose to become leader of the PC and as a vocal opponent of President Alfonso López Pumarejo's reformist and secularist programme, known as the *Revolución en Marcha* (Revolution in Progress). Educated at a Jesuit school in Bogota, Laureano Gómez was profoundly affected by Catholicism and the Jesuits. As PC leader, Laureano Gómez's discourse became increasingly ultramontane as he set about forging an alliance with the Catholic Church in opposition to the PL's New Deal that he associated with atheist freemasonry. As far as Laureano Gómez was concerned, the liberal reformists in government were threatening to take Colombia somewhere between Mexico and Russia.[4] However, as leader of the PC during the 1930s, and despite him being an outspoken admirer of Iberian authoritarianism and supporter of Franco during the Spanish civil war, Laureano Gómez kept the party within the democratic political sphere. As PC leader, he was also both an ally and a critic of the Leopardos, which was the closest movement to fascism in Colombia during the 1930s. Conservative Catholic values were perhaps the most consistent in his political life, with his attitude towards dictatorial regimes always shaped by their position towards the Church.[5]

What was done in other countries of 1930s Latin America under the ideological and institutional umbrella of corporatism, was carried out in Colombia by progressive liberals. While social corporatism became associated with the New Deal in some other countries of Latin America, in Colombia progressive liberals used this association and were the main actors driving the expansion of the state's social role in the face of fierce opposition from the PC and the Catholic Church.

Colombia began approaching the labour question while under conservative rule during the 1920s. In 1924, a National Labour Bureau (Oficina General del Trabajo) was created, and then in 1926, the first Labour Code was produced. However, it was only under Alfonso López Pumarejo's liberal governments (1934–38) that the 'incorporation' of labour took place.[6] With increasing polarization provoked by Laureano Gómez's opposition PC abstention policy that led to the boycott of elections and institutions, the PL government began the Revolution in Progress.[7] An admirer of Roosevelt's New Deal in the US, López Pumarejo introduced a social reformist programme that expanded social welfare, state intervention, promoted trade unions, and even introduced a modest agrarian reform – all of which were attacked by the conservatives.[8]

This programme, which led to López Pumarejo being called the 'Roosevelt of the Andes', shaped the 1936 constitutional revision. Social rights were incorporated into the Constitution and complemented by new laws in 1937 and 1938.[9] With state support, trade union membership increased significantly. Some articles drew their inspiration from the Mexican Constitution and from Léon Duguit, 'whose solidarist philosophy of the socialist saviour fired the imagination of progressive-minded Colombian liberals'.[10] Facing the clear and radical opposition of the PC and the suspicion of some PL centrists, López Pumarejo supported the creation of the Colombian Workers' Confederation (CTC – Confederación de Trabajadores de Colombia). The PL even provided some of the funding for the CTC's second congress, with this left-wing confederation – which was controlled by liberals, anarcho-syndicalists, and communists – becoming the dominant element of social bargaining in Colombia. However, this liberal hegemony provoked a shift towards the right of employers' associations, as can be seen with the creation of the National Patriotic Economic Action (APEN – Acción Patriótica Económica Nacional) in 1934 as a way to unite rural landowners, industrialists, and financiers.[11]

The secularizing nature of the 1936 constitutional revision did nothing to bring social Catholic corporatists any closer to supporting liberal policies. Abolishing Catholicism as the state religion and its dominance in education, the revision brought the Catholic Church and Laureano Gómez closer in their denunciation of the PL government as an 'atheist, Protestant and socialist leviathan'.[12]

As in other Latin American countries, Catholicism pre-empted the cultural spread of social and political corporatism. The Catholic Church and its charity and elite education institutions were important for introducing corporatism to Colombia. In the 1930s, the clear cultural convergence of Laureano Gómez and the Catholic Church cemented the opposition to liberal secularism and social reform. The fascists secular or technocratic-modernizing versions, while present within elite political culture, were overshadowed by the Catholic hegemony. Félix Restrepo and other Jesuits were important in spreading the ideas of social and authoritarian political corporatism, and were close to the CP throughout the 1930s, playing an important role in the failed reforms of 1950–53.[13] Restrepo was perhaps the most important supporter of corporatism, both in his writings and the positions he held at the Javeriana University, in Catholic associations and through his political and intellectual proximity to members of the conservative elite.[14] The hegemony of liberal, reformist and secularist governments in Colombia during the 1930s led to the dominance of corporatist ideologies that in the Iberian models found a conservative corporatist reaction to both liberalism and secular fascism. While the Spanish corporatism of Primo de Rivera and the polarization of the Spanish civil war had a profound effect on the political culture within the CP, and on Laureano Gómez in particular, Salazar's Portuguese model and his 1933 Constitution were among those mentioned most positively in the Catholic press, including *Revista Javeriana*.[15]

In common with other Catholic ideologues, Restrepo legitimized his corporatism in Thomist teachings and the social doctrine of the encyclicals. He was creative in seeking to avoid the accusations of statism levelled at him by his critics, often seeking refuge in his imagined model of the Catholic dictator, Salazar.[16] Offering corporatism as an alternative to liberalism and communism, Restrepo opposed the creation of a single party; rather, he called for the powers of political parties to be diluted through the creation of corporatist institutions.[17] In the early 1940s, he once more denied any link between corporatism and fascism.[18] While Laureano Gómez's constitutional reform was underway in 1951, Restrepo held a number of radio debates that were discussed by the commission responsible for the reform.[19]

As was the case throughout most of Latin America during the 1930s, Colombia witnessed the emergence of small fascist groups that included corporatism as an important part of their programme; however, most of them – with the exception of the Leopardos – survived 'sin pena ni gloria'.[20] The Leopardos, which became a fascist-oriented faction within the CP and often dissented from the party, emerged in the 1920s as a small elitist group influenced by Action Française, quickly expressing its criticism of Laureano Gómez's leadership of the CP. As one of its founders later wrote, 'All twentieth-century counter-revolutionary movements were born with Charles Maurras'.[21]

Its authoritarian stance, inspired by Action Française and Benito Mussolini, was already apparent in its 1924 nationalist manifesto; nevertheless, it still retained an important Catholic integralist base that led it to attack both the 'red menace' and some of the leaders of the PC.[22] The original group of members consisted of young traditionalist students who in the following decade radicalized the route to fascism in a political system dominated by the PL and its policies of social reform. The integral corporatism of traditionalism and fascism was at the heart of its political model throughout the 1930s, and especially of its anti-democratic nature, which contrasted with the 'true Colombia [of the] corporatist state, organized on eternal bases and natural units: the family, the municipality and the syndicate or corporation'.[23] In 1936, they formed Popular Nationalist Action (ANP – Acción Nacionalista Popular) and what was perhaps the most important dissident movement, the Rightist National Action (AND – Acción Nacional Derechista). It was not until he became leader of the CP in 1932 that Laureano Gómez distanced himself from them in his book *El Cuadrilatero: Mussolini – Hitler – Stalin – Gandhi*, in which he attacked both fascism and communism.[24] Despite this, relations between Laureano Gómez and the Leopardos were often close. While the latter adopted the strategy that he is not an 'enemy of the right' and one of its leaders, Silvio Villegas, claimed that his manifesto viewed corporatism as a means to revitalize the PC while simultaneously pushing for the violent overthrow of the PL government. At the PC's 1937 national conference, tensions between Laureano Gómez's Civilist group and the nationalists, who were close to fascism, were particularly clear.[25]

Nevertheless, while they did exercise some influence, the Leopardos never dominated the PC.[26] At the 1939 elections they presented independent lists and conducted an openly fascist campaign, but their results were very poor. The corporatism of the 1930s was, therefore, the most important legacy of the authoritarian political culture that was present in some sections of the PC in the context of the 1940s crises, although its fascist version was supported only by a minority.[27]

On the eve of the Second World War, the US had neither the same troubles with nor any need to exert the same anti-Axis diplomatic pressures on Colombia as it had to in other Latin American countries. PL leaders established strong strategic alliances with the US, and President Eduardo Santos Montejo was the leading author of Colombian-US cooperation.[28] While in many other Latin American countries a democratizing wave was in motion by 1945, in Colombia there were clear signs that its oligarchic democracy was eroding and making way for a powerful wave of inter-party violence (La Violencia), riots, increased factionalism, and the appearance of populist leaders.

It was in this context of escalating violence and polarization, of the assassination of populist politicians like Jorge Eliécer Gaitán Ayala, and the breakdown of negotiations between the PC and the PL that in November 1949 Conservative President Luis Mariano Ospina Pérez declared a state of siege, closed the PL-dominated Congress and suspended civil liberties. Laureano Gómez, a rival of Mariano Ospina Pérez within the PC, then had the chance to become president of Colombia, standing as the only candidate in an election that was boycotted by the liberals, and already in an authoritarian setting. During his short dictatorship, Laureano Gómez did not challenge the alliance with the US. Despite his initial suspicion of North American diplomacy and his criticism of the PL's close relationship with Washington during the Second World War, Colombia became a military ally of the US during the Korean War.[29]

President Laureano Gómez's corporatist solution did not come by surprise, even when considering just the early 1940s. In 1942, when he gave up his seat in the Senate, Laureano Gómez began defending a mixed system of representation in the context of crisis, a position he reaffirmed after the *Bogotazo* (the riots that broke out after Jorge Eliécer Gaitán's assassination in April 1948). In 1943, he stated that 'in my design, corporatism is not an opponent of democracy [...] it fits it economically [...] a parliament such as we have now [...] cannot perform'.[30] In 1948, in a speech in Franco's Spain, he mentioned the positive aspects of organic representation since democracy was 'incapable of halting [...] the communist revolution'.[31]

Laureano Gómez was not alone in promoting corporatist projects for reforming political institutions: liberals such as Rafael Víctor Zenón Uribe and Gaitán had previously endorsed the idea of transforming the Senate into a corporatist body or a 'working chamber': an alternative to a 'chamber of politicians', in the words of Uribe.[32] These projects resurfaced in the context of the crisis of the 1940s. In 1942, Gaitán was even invited to lead a technocratic parliament.[33] The conservative Rafael Bernal Jiménez also presented a project in 1943 that would provide representation of professions in a parliament in which guilds would act as co-legislators, removing some of its legislative nature from it.[34]

Laureano Gómez outlined his authoritarian constitutional reform project in a message to Congress and carefully followed the work of the Constitutional Commission (CEC – Comisión de Estudios Constitucionales) that led the proposal. The message was clear: to remove the 'profanity' of the democratic principle of '50 per cent plus one'.[35] The PL refused to take part in the CEC and boycotted the constitutional assembly (ANAC – Asamblea Nacional Constituyente) that was to approve it. In addition to representatives from political parties, ANAC also had organic representatives, including business owners, trade unions, universities, and other institutions.

The CEC debates were dominated by Laureano Gómez's PC group and Rafael Bernal Jiménez, a conservative professor of law and education, who was the leading promoter of the 1953 corporatist reform, despite rejecting this term which, he believed, 'could be interpreted in bad faith'.[36] Restrepo, the leading promoter of corporatism in the news media at this time, was appointed to the CEC, but because he had left for Mexico he did not get involved in its workings.[37] The CEC discussed several constitutions at length and carefully studied proposals submitted by Restrepo, as well as suggestions provided by the Episcopal Conference to the Archbishop of Bogota.[38]

The final draft established the president's autonomy and power, increased the presidential mandate and the president's independence from the legislature, restricted the separation of powers, abolished part of the law of separation of church and state contained in the PL's 1936 constitutional revision, introduced double suffrage for heads of family in certain elections and, above all, turned the Senate into a corporatist-style consultative chamber.

The main novelty of this constitutional reform was, without doubt, the return of the Catholic Church to the state sphere and corporatism.

The family, as the primary cell of society, and the syndicate as units of employers and workers introduced the organic concept of society into the Constitution, with the state becoming increasingly confessional. Catholicism once more received state protection and special access to public education and several other institutions, following the model of the Iberian dictatorships. The new Senate, which was transformed into a consultative body, included fifteen senators elected by an electoral college of municipal councils in addition to those whose positions were the result of corporatist representation: commercial, industrial, and agricultural associations; syndicates from the same sectors; universities; church; and liberal professionals.[39] The new Constitution also created a National Economic Council (CEN – Consejo Económico Nacional) that was responsible for advising the president on economic matters. Such bodies existed in several other Latin American constitutions of the 1930s.[40] With the CEN, the president's ability to intervene in matters of economic planning increased.[41]

It is also worth noting that this new corporatist representation emerged in a dictatorial context, with the large preponderance of employer's interests, a weakened CTC and with the Union of Colombian Workers (UTC – Unión de Trabajadores de Colombia), which was formed at the 1946 Episcopal Conference and was controlled by the Catholic Church Social Action, as a the candidate to occupy this place within the new corporatist structure.[42]

The new Constitution was a legacy of the 1930s culture of authoritarian conservatism, and the final project was criticized by other PC leaders for not representing 'the country's democratic and civil traditions'.[43] Nevertheless, Laureano Gómez remained convinced this new Constitution would ensure Colombia could remain free of universal suffrage, violence, and communism.[44] Despite the strong cultural connections between Laureano Gómez and Franco's Spain, the constitutional model of Portugal was closest to his project. On the other hand, in 1952 there was already a large number of authoritarian constitutions in Europe and Latin America that could be emulated.

Gómez, however, had no time to approve the Constitution before he was overthrown by Colombia's first military coup of the twentieth century. Unable to control the spread of violence and facing opposition to his authoritarian plans from within his own party, Laureano Gómez fell in 1953 to a military coup supported by the PL and conservatives from the *Ospinista* wing of the party. Led by General Rojas Pinilla, who Laureano Gómez rejected as war minister in his government, the new military regime promised an end to the *violencia* and to pull back from authoritarianism.

In Colombia, the most important groups in the spread of corporatism were, therefore, associated with the conservative and Catholic world.[45] The Catholic Church pre-empted this diffusion and in the case of Colombia its dominant characteristic was more evident. While there were more secular variations in existence, ranging from the fascist to the more technocratic, the domination of Laureano Gómez's Catholic and Hispanic influence was evident both within Catholic organizations and the PC. It was also in the context of its hegemony of the PC during the 1930s that Colombian fascist corporatism emerged, although always as a minority trend.

Had it succeeded, Laureano Gómez's project could have consolidated a confessional and corporatist authoritarian regime. Inspired by 'the pre-1930 (Colombian) conservative regime and right-wing Iberian experiments, Laureano Gómez proclaimed an austere counterrevolution in which the present would be securely anchored to the past, and cherished values of hierarchy, stability and religion would be reaffirmed'.[46]

Notes

1 H. H. Figueroa Salamanca, 'Um projeto corporativo na Colômbia: Laureano Gómez entre os grémios económicos e o clero (1934–1952)', in Pinto and Martinho, eds., *A Onda Corporativa*, pp. 327–44.
2 E. Posada Carbó, ed., *Colombia: Mirando Hacia Dentro (1930–1960)*, Madrid, Fundación MAPFRE-Taurus, 2015.
3 A. W. Wilde, 'Conversations among gentlemen: Oligarchical democracy in Colombia', in J. J. Linz and A. Stepan, eds., *The Breakdown of Democratic Regimes: Latin America*, Baltimore, MD, Johns Hopkins University Press, 1978, p. 28.
4 Cit. in C. Abel and P. Marco, 'Colombia, 1930–58', in L. Bethell, ed., *The Cambridge History of Latin America*, Cambridge, Cambridge University Press, 1991, p. 603.
5 J. D. Henderson, *Conservative Thought in Twentieth Century Latin America: The Ideas of Laureano Gómez*, Athens, OH, Monographs in International studies, 1988; J. Guerrero Barón, *El Proceso Político de las Derechas en Colombia y los Imaginários sobre las Guerras Internacionales, 1930–1945*, Tunja, Universidad Pedagógica y Tecnológica de Colombia, 2014, p. 252.
6 On the OGT, see O. Gallo, 'Instituições laborais e intervencionismo social na Colômbia, 1923–1946', *Anuario Colombiano de Historia Social y de la Cultura*, Volume 43, Number 2, 2016, pp. 335–60. See Collier and Collier, *Shaping the Political Arena*, pp. 289–313.
7 See R. Arias Trujillo, *Historia de Colombia Contemporánea (1920–2010)*, Bogotá, Universidad de los Andes, 2011, pp. 57–83.
8 Ó. Mora Toscano, 'Los dos gobiernos de Alfonso López Pumarejo: Estado y reformas económicas y sociales en Colombia (1934–1938, 1942–1945)', *Apuntes del CENES*, Volume XXIX, Number 50, 2010, pp. 151–71.

9 J. D. Henderson, *Modernization in Colombia: The Laureano Gómez Years, 1889–1965*, Gainesville, University Press of Florida, 2001, p. 229.
10 Cit. in Henderson, Ibid., p. 229. See also A. M. Mercado Gazabón, *La Influencia de León Duguit en la Reforma Social de 36 en Colombia: El Sistema Jurídico, la Función Social de la Propriedad y la Teoría de los Servicios Públicos*, Bogotá, Editorial de la Universidad del Rosario, 2015.
11 H. Figueroa Salamanca and C. Tuta Alarcón, 'El estado corporativo colombiano: Una propuesta de derechas, 1930–1953', *Anuario Colombiano de Historia Social y de la Cultura*, Volume 32, 2005, pp. 99–148.
12 D. Turriago Rojas, 'La actitud de la Iglesia Católica colombiana durante las hegemonias liberal y conservadora de 1930 a 1953', *Cuestiones Teológicas*, Volume 44, Number 101, 2017, p. 76.
13 On his role in 1950, see J. D. Henderson, 'El proyeto de reforma constitucional conservadora de 1953 en Colombia', *Anuario Colombiano de Historia Social y de la Cultura*, Volumes 13–14, 1986, p. 270. See also J. Beltrán Alvarado, 'Cuando se borró el nombre de Dios: Laureano Gómez, Félix Restrepo S. J. Y el proyecto corporativista colombiano (1930–1946)', master's thesis, Pontefícia Universidad Javeriana, Bogota, 2018.
14 Restrepo, *Corporativismo*.
15 Among several exemples of articles, see the ones by the jesuit C. Lara, 'El nuevo estado corporativo português', *Revista Javeriana*, Volume 39, 1937, pp. 276–88, and Volume 40, 1937, pp. 363–71. The above cited book by Joaquín Azpiazu, *El Estado Corporativo*, was widely discussed in Colombia.
16 F. Restrepo, 'Corporativismo de estado y corporativismo gremial', *Revista Javeriana*, Volume 49, 1938, pp. 224–35.
17 Ibid.
18 F. Restrepo, 'Corporativismo no es fascismo', *La Razon*, 19 June 1944, p. 2.
19 F. Restrepo, *Colombia en la Encrucijada*, Bogota, Ministerio de Educación Nacional, 1951.
20 J. C. Ruiz Vásquez, *Leopardos y Tempestades: Historia del Fascismo en Colombia*, Bogota, Javegraf, 2004, p. 132.
21 Cit. in R. Arias Trujillo, 'Las derechas en Colombia durante los años 1920', in Bohoslavsky, Jorge and Lida, eds., *Las Derechas Ibero-Americanas*, 2019.
22 For more about the origins of the Leopardos, see R. Arias Trujillo, *'Los Leopardos': Una Historia Intelectual de los años 1920*, Bogota, Universidad de los Andes, 2007.
23 Cit. in J. A. Hernández, 'Los Leopardos y el fascismo en Colombia', *Historia y Comunicación Social*, Volume 5, 2000, pp. 224–5.
24 L. Gómez, *El Cuadrilátero: Mussolini – Hitler – Stalin – Gandhi*, Bogota, Editorial Centro, 1935.
25 S. Villegas, *No Hay Enemigos a la Derecha (Materiales para una Teoría Nacionalista)*, Manizales, A. Zapata, 1937. See also Vásquez, *Leopardos y Tempestades*, p. 136.
26 Vasquéz, Ibid., p. 151.
27 J. Gaitán-Bohórquez and M. Malagón-Pinzón, 'Fascismo y autoritarismo en Colombia', *Vniversitas*, Volume 118, 2009, pp. 293–316.
28 See B. L. Coleman, *Colombia and the United States: The Making of an Inter-American Alliance, 1939–1960*, Kent, OH, Kent State University Press, 2008.

29 Coleman, *Colombia and the United States*, p. 74.
30 Cit. in Barón, *El Proceso Político*, p. 369.
31 Cit. in Henderson, *Modernization in Colombia*, p. 353.
32 Henderson, Ibid., p. 253.
33 Ibid., p. 289.
34 D. N. Prado Motta, *Laureano Gómez Castro y su Proyecto de Reforma Constitucional* (1951–1953), Bogota, Editorial Universidad del Rosario, 2008, p. 126.
35 Cit. in Henderson, 'El Proyeto de Reforma Constitucional', p. 274.
36 Cit. in Motta, *Laureano Gómez Castro*, p. 125. See also R. Bernal Jiménez, *La Cuestión Social y la Lucha de Clases*, Bogota, Editorial Centro, 1940, and especially, *Hacia una Democracia Orgánica*, Madrid, Afrodisio Aguado, 1951.
37 A. Cacua Prada, *Félix Restrepo S. J.*, Bogotá, Instituto Caro y Cuervo, 1997, p. 196.
38 Especially F. Restrepo, *Colombia en la Encrucijada*. On the debates on the corporatist representation, see Motta, *Laureano Gómez Castro*, pp. 124–35, and, especially, Ministerio del Gobierno, *Estudios Constitucionales*, 2 vols., Bogota, Imprenta Nacional, 1953.
39 Motta, *Laureano Gómez Castro*, p. 130.
40 See Pinto, 'Authoritarianism and corporatism in Latin America', in Pinto and Finchelstein, eds., *Authoritarianism and Corporatism in Europe and Latin America*, pp. 118–31.
41 For the relations between the modernizing plans of the Lauchlin Currie Mission of the World Bank and the constitutional reform projects, see M. Malagón Pinzón and D. N. Pardo Motta, 'Laureano Gómez, la Misión Currie y el proyecto de reforma constitucional de 1952', *Criterio Jurídico*, Volume 9, Number 2, 2009, pp. 29–31.
42 H. H. Figueroa Salamanca, *Tradicionalismo, Hispanismo y Corporativismo: Una Aproximación a las Relaciones non Sanctas entre Religión y Política en Colombia (1930–1952)*, Bogota, Editorial Bonaventuriana, 2009.
43 M. T. Cifuentes Traslaviña, 'El catolicismo intransigente, elemento esencial del pensamiento conservador de Laureano Gómez', *Ensayos Críticos*, Number 4, 2008, p. 91.
44 L. Gómez, *Los Efectos de la Reforma de 1953*, Bogota, Imprenta Nacional, 1953.
45 Figueroa Salamanca, *Tradicionalismo, Hispanismo y Corporativismo*.
46 Abel and Marco, 'Colombia, 1930–58', pp. 621–2.

13 The 'fascist era' in Latin America: the resilience of competitive authoritarianism
Concluding remarks

During the 1930s, a wave of dictatorships swept over Latin America, each adopting new authoritarian institutions that were created in the political laboratory of the inter-war world, particularly the personalization of leadership, the single or dominant party, and the 'organic-statist' legislatures based on corporatist models. Latin America participated in what has been called the first wave of democratization and in the subsequent 'reverse wave' of the inter-war period. Corporatism had its first global moment during this period and Latin America was an integral part of this political dynamic.[1]

In this book – a comparative-historical analysis with a 'case oriented' perspective – we have dealt with the successes and failures of the institutional reform processes in selected authoritarian regimes in Latin America during the 1930s. We paid particular attention to how domestic political elites pursued similar authoritarian changes while looking at institutional models of corporatism for their own countries.[2] In fact, it seems clear that the majority of these regimes did 'undergo, simultaneously, a political-economic and a legal-political transformation, which led to the emergence of regimes with pronounced corporatist features'.[3]

Claiming legitimacy through organic views of society, they partially incorporated organized labour into the state, simultaneously offering workers constitutional recognition of collective socio-material rights while attempting a new type of (corporatist) political representation in the configuration of the new political systems.

The common analytical structure of the cases enabled us to single out the three main axes of the institutionalization (or absence thereof) marking the majority of the contemporaneous dictatorships: attempts to create a single or dominant party; the institutionalization of social and political corporatism; and the presence of dominant models that were developed by the intellectual-politicians who were involved in them (Table 13.1). Since representation is an essential element of modern

Table 13.1 Authoritarian Regimes, Parties, and Corporatism in Latin America

Country	Regime	Single and/or Dominant Party	Social Corporatism	Political Corporatism
Argentina	Uriburu (1930–32)	No	No	Yes
Bolivia	David Toro (1936–37)	Partido Socialista del Estado	Yes	Yes
	Germán Busch (1937–39)	No	Yes	No
Brazil	Getúlio Vargas (1937–1945)	Legião Cívica Nacional[a]	Yes	Yes
Chile	Ibañéz del Campo (1927–31)	Confederación Republicana de Acción Cívica de Obreros y Empleados	Yes	Yes (CRAC in Parliament)
Colombia	Carlos Dávila Espinoza (1932)	No	Yes	Yes
	Laureano Goméz (1950–53)	No	No	Yes
México	Lázaro Cárdenas (1934–40)	Partido de la Revolución Mexicana	Yes	Yes
Paraguay	Rafael Franco (1936–37)	Union Nacional Revolucionária	Yes	Yes (Constitution of 1940)
Peru	Estegarrabia (1937–40)	No	Yes	Yes
	Sánchez Cerro (1931–33)	Union Revolucionária	Yes	Yes
	Oscar Benavides (1933–39)	No	No	No
Uruguay	Gabriel Terra (1933–38)	No	No	Partial (Constitution of 1934)
	Alfredo Baldomir (1938–42)	No	No	No

a Never created.

political systems, authoritarian regimes tended to create political institutions in which the function of corporatism was to legitimate organic representation and ensure the co-optation and control of sections of the elite and organized interests. Our focus on political institutions associated with political and social corporatism has captured a rich array of entanglements between authoritarian political actors, and we also emphasize the impact of political learning and diffusion from seemingly successful institutional innovations and precedents elsewhere.

Corporatism permeated the main political families and elites of the conservative and authoritarian political right and of supporters of technocratic governments associated with state-led modernization policies in both Europe and Latin America during the inter-war period. However, in the Latin American case, the conservative and reactionary Catholic intellectual-politicians tended to be the ones who promoted corporatist alternatives by synthesizing fascist and social Catholic options, which were often shaped by the interventionist options associated with the 1929 crisis. It is in this context that Catholic authoritarian intellectual-politicians crossed the Atlantic Ocean and the borders of Latin America on a number of occasions, adopting models that were readily available on the Iberian Peninsula, such as those of Miguel Primo de Rivera in Spain and Oliveira Salazar in Portugal.

The Catholic press gave voice to an impressive process that spread social and political corporatist ideas associated mainly with Iberia throughout Latin America, thereby avoiding association with Italian Fascism. When we examine the corpus of the new authoritarian nationalist constructs in Brazil, Argentina, Chile, Peru, and many other Latin American countries, we see the influence of Action Française blended with the corresponding Iberian elite movements – Acción Española in Spain and Integralismo Lusitano in Portugal. For example, the Argentinian nationalists were the main creators of an authoritarian version of Argentinian national identity: one that was corporatist, Catholic, Hispanic, and which placed great stock on values such as hierarchy, anti-liberalism, and anti-communism.

To emphasize the instrumental and transitory nature of his authoritarianism in Brazil, Oliveira Viana differentiated his project from the Italian Fascist model, stressing the technical-juridical nature of his approach and restating both Manoïlesco and the New Deal jurists, while all the time maintaining the authoritarian model. Many of the other Latin American intellectual-politicians who collaborated closely with the dictators that were associated with the institutionalization of corporatism in Latin America hailed from this cultural background.

In the world of inter-war dictatorships, however, both the single (and/or dominant party) and the corporatist bodies became the backbone for the institutionalization of these regimes.[4] In almost all authoritarian regime institutionalization processes during this period, the attempt to create a party to help the dictator consolidate his position, soon became the Achilles' heel of the institutional reform process. Usually the product of conservative coalitions supported by military coups, it was generally the resilience of the liberal conservative parties that prevented them from consolidating. In fact, party politics remained central to the institutional arrangements, with many of these regimes being unable to consolidate, and with them remaining mixed forms of competitive authoritarianism with limited pluralism and elections characterized by large-scale abuses of state power, although with formal democratic institutions that remained the principal means of legitimacy.[5] That was the case of the 'infamous decade' in Argentina and Peru after Sánchez Cerro. In Chile, Ibañéz was resisted by the parties, and following a series of complex negotiations, the regime party failed to became a central part of the political arena of that period with its existence being cut short when Ibañéz stood down as President in 1931. Elsewhere, the 'state of exception' was the norm, with the suspension of elections and of parliaments.

The attempts to create official parties multiplied, but they remained diverse in nature. The dominant model was to construct them from above, based on a more or less forced winning unification. In Paraguay, Stefanich, who had emerged as the strong man of the government, was the main figure behind the creation of the UNR as the new regime's official party in November 1936, becoming the first president of a party that had been created at the 'invitation' of the dictator, Rafael Franco. In Bolívia, Toro tried to create a dominant party, the PSE. In Peru, Sánchez Cerro created the UR. Vargas's New State in Brazil was perhaps the only regime to consolidate without a party. The LCN suffered opposition from many members of the regional elite, and Vargas feared any new party could create a focus for tensions that could weaken his hold on power.

The 'corporatist parties', such as Ibañéz's CRAC, were in the minority. A blend of corporatist institution and political party, and with parliamentary representation, CRAC served as a representative body alongside the parties in a controlled congress. The exception was the paradigmatic case of Cárdenas's PRM in Mexico, the only dominant 'corporatist' party to consolidate, although with political origins and ideological legitimacy that was very different from those mentioned above, being closer to a nationalism, secularism, and developmentalism that was associated with the left of the political spectrum.

The 1929 crisis worsened some elements of the crises of liberal-democratic regimes, although with different impacts. Like with Europe, it was not easy to find in the Great Depression the determining factor for the rise of authoritarianism. There was, in fact, a wider range of variation. What was carried out in the authoritarian regimes of the 1930s Latin America under the ideological and institutional umbrella of corporatism was done so by liberal-democratic regimes and progressive liberals, as in Colombia and Chile. While social corporatism became associated with the New Deal in some countries of Latin America, in Colombia progressive liberals used this association to drive forward with the expansion of the state's social role in the face of strong opposition from the Conservative Party and the Catholic Church.

The New Deal, as 'a national version of a larger pattern' was a variant of the responses to the 1929 crisis, which challenged the response of the corporatists to the crisis. This later became the dominant model of state-interest group relations, especially with labour in Latin American regimes.[6] Of course, transfers and transnational connections were on the move, and some of the icons of the New Deal, particularly the creation of state regulation agencies, were also adopted by authoritarian regimes. To avoid association with Italian Fascism and other European dictatorships, like those in Spain and Portugal, the political discourse associating the institutionalization of social corporatism with the New Deal was often used as a political legitimation of authoritarianism; however, while social corporatism suppressed independent labour organizations with state control, using them as instruments of state policy, this did not happen in Chile or Colombia under López Pumarejo. In fact, in Colombia some of the institutional arrangements were introduced while maintaining a restricted democracy.

In 1943, in one of the many accounts of the spread of corporatism during the 'fascist era', Mario Gianturco underlined the relationship between social and political corporatism in Latin America was as in Europe. In Brazil, as elsewhere, the problem of the corporatist organization of the national economy has been dominated by the reaction to parliamentarism, namely by the degeneration of the representative system, and by the need to ensure a stable and strong government.[7] Latin America in the 1930s was integrated into that wave.

Notes

1 S. Reichardt, 'The global circulation of corporatism: Concluding remarks', in Pinto and Finchelstein, eds., *Authortarianism and Corporatism*, p. 275.

2 The Colliers called it the 'case' rather than 'variable' oriented approach to comparative-historical analysis, one that is mainly concerned with how each variable is embedded in its larger context within a given case. See Collier and Collier, *Shaping the Political Arena*, p. 173.
3 Thornhill, 'The rise and fall of corporatism constitutionalism', in Pinto, ed., *Corporatism and Fascism*, p. 78.
4 Here 'dominant party' is defined as 'a political institution that has the leading role in determining access to most political offices, shares powers over policymaking and patronage distribution, and uses privileged access to state resources or extra-constitutional means to maintain its position in power'. From Flores-Macías, 'México's PRI: The resilience of an authoritarian successor party and its consequences for democracy', in Loxton and Mainwaring, eds., *Life after Dictatorship*, p. 260.
5 See J. Mahoney, *The Legacies of Liberalism. Path dependence and political regimes in Central America*, Baltimore, The Johns Hopkins University Press, 2001.
6 Patel, *The New Deal*, p. 7.
7 Mario Gianturco, *Il volto corporativo della nuova Europa*, Milan, Fratelli Bocca, 1943, p. 343, cit. in Pasetti, 'From Rome to Latin America', in Pinto and Finchelstein, eds., *Authoritarianism and Corporatism*, p. 158.

Index

1929 crisis 21, 28, 31, 47, 62, 110, 112

Abascal Infante, Salvador 91–2
Action Française 9, 17, 19, 33, 48, 101, 110
Agorio, Adolfo 64
Aguirre Cerda, Pedro 44
Alessandri, Arturo 41–2
Amaral, Azevedo 72
Andrade, Varela de 64
Archbishop of Bogota 103
Argaña, Luis 56
Argentina: 1930 coup 31; 1931 manifesto 35; Alianza Nacionalista Argentina (ANA) 36; anti-Semitism 33; *Criterio* 19; Federación Nacional Democrática (FND) 34–5; *Hispanidad* 33; Irazusta brothers 19, 32; Legión Cívica Argentina (LCA) 32, 36; Peronism 37; provincial interventors 34; Sáenz Peña Law 31–2; Unión Cívica Radical (UCR) 31; Uriburismo 36
Arias, Gino 33
Ayala, Eusebio 53
Azpiazu, Joaquín 18, 33

Baldomir, Afredo 28, 62–5
Barroso, Gustavo 64, 70
Batista, Fulgencio 29
Belaúnde, Víctor Andrés 48
Benavides, Óscar (General) 20, 28–9, 47–51
Bernal Jiménez, Rafael 103
Bolivia: 1936 coup 58; 1938 Constitution 60; 52-point programme 58; Asamblea Nacional Permanente de Organizaciones Sindicales 59; Busch Code 60; military socialist revolution 58; Partido Socialista del Estado (PSE) 60; social corporatism 59
Brazil: 1898 liberal Constitution 69; 1930 Revolution 68–9, 72, 74; 1932 Constitutionalist Revolt 69; 1934 Constitution 68–70; 1935 state of siege 69; 1937 Constitution 64, 68, 72, 75–6; 1937 Coup 71, 75; 1943 Consolidated Labour Laws 78; *A Ordem* 19; Ação Integralista Brasileira (AIB) 18, 20, 49, 64, 69–71, 75–6, 79; Aliança Nacional Libertadora (ANL) 69; Catholic Action 17, 74; Christian Democratic Party 18; Cohen Plan 69; Conselho da Economía Nacional (CEN) 75, 79; Departamento Administrativo do Serviço Público (DASP) 77; Departamento de Informação e Propaganda (DISP) 76; Estado Novo (New State) 8, 18, 27–9, 64, 68, 72, 77–9, 111; Federação das Indústrias do Estado de São Paulo (FIESP) 70; Guanabara Palace 71; *imposto sindical* 78; *interventores* 69, 76–7; Itamaraty Commission 73; Legião Cearense do Trabalho (LCT) 71; Legião Cívica Nacional (LCT) 76, 111; Ministério do Trabalho, Indústria e Comércio (MTIC) 70, 73; October Legion 72; Second World War 76, 79; Serviço Sindical Corporativo

116 Index

(SSC) 71; social corporatism 79; *tenentes* 68; *Trabalhismo* 79; União Revolucionária (UR) 20; US aid 79
Brena, Tomás G. 63
Bullrich, Miguel 18
Busch, Germán (Colonel) 20, 28, 58–60

Caballero, Bernardino 54
Calles, Elías 87–8
Camacho, Ávila 89
Campo, Ibañéz del 28
Campos, Francisco 71–3, 75–6
Capanema, Gustavo 72
Cárdenas, Lázaro 3, 28–9, 85–91, 111
Carulla, Juan 32, 35
Castilhos, Julio de 69
Catholic revival 19
Catholicism: social 17
Cerro, Sánchez 28–9
Chaco War 53, 58
Chile: 1924 military intervention 41; Christian Democratic Party 43; Confederación de la Producción y el Comercio (CPC) 44; Confederación Nacional de Sindicatos Legales (CNSL) 42; Confederación Republicana de Acción Cívica de Obreros y Empleados de Chile (CRAC) 42, 109, 111; Falange Nacional 22, 44; La Milicia Republicana (MR) 44; Movimiento Nacional Socialista Chileno (MNSC) 44; National Economic Council 43; Nueva Acción Pública (NAP) 43; Partido Agrario Laborista (PAL) 44; Partido Conservador 41–2; Popular Corporatist Party 44; Popular Front 44; Unión Popular (UP) 48
Colombia: 1930 elections 98; 1936 Constitution 99, 104; 1946 Episcopal Conference 104; 1949 state of siege 102; Acción Nacional Derechista (AND) 101; Acción Nacionalista Popular (ANP) 101; Acción Patriótica Económica Nacional (APEN) 100; Asamblea Nacional Constituyente 103; *Bogotazo* 102; Catholic Church 104, 112; Comisión de Estudios Constitucionales (CEC) 103; Confederación de Trabajadores de Colombia (CTC) 99, 104; Consejo Económico Nacional (CEN) 104; Episcopal Conference 103; Javeriana University 100; Jesuits 100; *La Violencia* 102; Leopardos 99, 101; New Deal 98; Oficina General del Trabajo (OGT) 99; Partido Conservador (PC) 98–104, 112; Partido Liberal Colombiano (PLC) 98–101, 103–4; *Revolución en Marcha* 98–9; Second World War 102; secularization 100, 103; Unión de Trabajadores de Colombia (UTC) 104; Unión de Trabajadores de Colombia (UTC) 104
corporatism 2–3, 64–5, 110; *corporatisme d'association* 10–11; social 74; (definition) 8; political (definition) 9

Dávila Espinoza, Carlos 28, 41, 43
democratization: reverse wave 108
Dollfuss, Englebert 63

Eguiguren, Luis Antonio 50
Eliécer Gaitán, Jorge 102
Esteves, Freire 54
Esteves, Gomes Freire 54
Estigarribia Insaurralde, José Félix (General) 28, 53–6
Eyzaguirre, Jaime 44

Federzoni, Luigi 65
Figueiredo, Jackson de 19
Figueroa, Emiliano 41
Filho, Alexandre Macondes 79
Flores, Luis A. 47–50
Fragoso, Tasso (General) 27
Franceschi, Gustavo (Monsignor) 18, 33
Franco, Francisco 93
Franco, Rafael (Colonel) 27–8, 53–4, 111
Frei, Eduardo 18, 44

Gaitán Ayala, Jorge Eliécer 102–3
Gaona, Francisco 54
Garretón, Manuel 18, 44
Germany: National Socialism 44; Weimar Constitution 48

Gianturco, Mario 112
Gómez Morín, Manuel 91–3, 104
Gómez, Juan Vicente 28
Gómez, Laureano 28, 101, 98–105; Civilist group 102
González Luna, Efraín 92–3
Great Depression 8, 27–8, 112

Hernández Martínez, Maximiliano (General) 29
hispanismo 18–19

Ibáñez del Campo, Carlos 28, 41–2, 111
Ibarguren, Carlos 32, 34–5
Irazusta, Julio 35
Irazusta, Rodolfo 35
Ireland: 1937 Constitution 10
Italy: Fascism 3, 17, 19–20, 33, 42, 58, 71, 76, 90, 110, 112; *Carta del Lavoro* (Labour Charter) 11, 20, 31, 49, 54, 76

Jesuits 18
Justo, Agustín Pedro (General) 31, 34–6

Korean War 102

Leguía, Augusto 27, 47
Leme, Sebastião (Cardinal) 18, 74–5
Lima, Alceu de Amoroso 75
Linz, Juan J. 12
Loewenstein, Karl 12
Lombardo Toledano, Vicente 87
López Pumarejo 19, 31–5, 98–9, 112; Roosevelt of the Andes 99

Maeztu, Ramiro de 19, 33
Manoilescu, Mihail 7, 74, 93, 110
Marquis de La Tour du Pin 11
Maurras, Charles 22, 33, 71, 101
Meinvielle, Julio (Father) 33
Mexico: 1917 Constitution 60, 86; 1931 Federal Labour Law 86, 92; 1938 Constituent Congress 88; 1938 rebellion 90; Acción Revolucionaria Mexicanista (ARM) 90; BASE 91–2; Camisas Doradas 90; Catholic Action 91; Catholic Cristiada 90; Chambers of Commerce and Industry Law 89; Confederación Católica del Trabajo (CCT) 92–3; Confederación de Cámaras Industriales (CONCAMIM) 89; Confederación de Cámaras Nacionales de Comercio, Servicios y Turismo (CONCANACO) 89; Confederación de las Clases Medias (CCM) 90–1; Confederación de Trabajadores Mexicanos (CTM) 87–9; Corporatist Catholicism 91; *dictablanda* 86; Green Shirts 92: *hispanismo* 90, 93; Jacobinism 90; *La Nación* 93; Liga Nacional de la Defensa de la Libertad de la Religión 8, 53, 92; National Assembly 93; nationalization of oil 86; Partido Comunista de México (PCM) 87; Partido de Acción Nacional (PAN) 91–3; Partido de la Revolución Mexicana (PRM) 85–90, 94, 111; 1933 Querétaro convention 87; Partido Revolucionario Institucional (PRI) 86–7; Revolution 86; Sexenal Plan 87; Single Labour Front 87; social corporatism 90; Unión Nacional Sinarquista (UNS) 20, 90–3
Morínigo, Higinio 56
Motta, Jeová 71
Mussolini, Benito 8, 36, 49, 59, 65, 101

New Deal 21, 28, 74, 110, 112

Ospina Pérez, Luis Mariano 102

Paiva, Félix 55
Palma, Arturo Alessandri 43
Pan-Latinism 20
Paraguay: 1936 agrarian reform law 54; 1940 Constitution 55; Asociacion Nacional de Ex-Combatientes (ANEC) 55; Colorado Party 55, 62–5; Confederacion Paraguaya de Trabajadores (CPT) 54; Decree-Law 152, 53; Febrerismo 53–4; February Revolution 55; Liga Nacional Independiente (LNI) 53;

118 Index

National Constituent Convention 55; Partido Nacional Revolucionario (PNR) 54; *Tiempistas* 55–6; Unión Nacional Revolucionaria (UNR) 54
Perón, Juan (General) 37
Peru: 1933 Constitution 50; Acción Patriótica (AP) 49; *Acción* 49; Alianza Popular Revolucionaria Americana (APRA) 47–50; Consejo de Economía Nacional (CEN) 48; *fuerzas vivas* 50; Ministry of Public Health, Labour and Social Welfare 50; Partido Comunista Peruano (PCP) 47; Partido Nacionalista (PN) 49; Unión Revolucionaria (UR) 20, 47–50, 111
Pesch, Heirich 12
Poland: 1935 Constitution 75; Pilsudsky, Josef 75
Pope Pius X 17
Pope Pius XI 8
Pope Pius XII 12
Popular Front 89
Portugal: 1933 Constitution 75; Integralismo Lusitano 19, 71, 110; Liga de Ação Universal Corporativa 8; New State 49, 55, 74–5; Salazar, António de Oliveira 18, 33, 36, 55, 63, 93, 101, 110; Salazarism 8; Sardinha, António 71; Secretariado para a Propaganda Nacional (SPN) 76
Primo de Rivera, Miguel 3, 8, 17, 19, 32, 41, 62, 90, 93, 110
Pumarejo, López 28

Quadragesimo Anno 8, 12, 17

Ramos, Juan P. 31
Reale, Miguel 20, 70–1
Rerum Novarum 8, 12, 17, 21, 91
Restrepo, Félix 18, 100–3; Thomism 100
Riva-Agüero, José de la 19, 48–9
Rojas Pinilla, Gustavo (General) 98, 104
Roman Catholic Church 7, 8, 17; French Cardinals 1936 letter 18

Salgado, Plínio 18, 20, 64, 70–1

Sánchez Cerro, Luis Miguel (Colonel) 27, 47–50, 111
Santos Montejo, Eduardo 102
Savarino, Franco 20
Sorondo, Sánchez 34, 36
Spain: Acción Española 19, 33, 48, 110; Falange 44; Somatén Nacional 32; Spanish Civil War 36, 90, 99–100
Spirito, Ugo 9
Stefanich, Juan 53–4

Terra, Gabriel 20, 27–9, 62–3, 65
Toledano, Vicente Lomardo 87–9
Toro, David (Colonel) 27–8, 58

Uriburu, José Félix 8, 20, 27–9, 31–2, 34–7
Uruguay: 1931 presidential elections 62; 1934 Constitution 62–5; 1935 revolt 63; 1940 Brena report 63; Acción Revisionista del Uruguay (ARU) 64; Colorado Party 63; Consejo Económico de la República (CER) 64; Consejo Nacional de Administración (CAN) 62; Consejo Superior de Trabajo (CST) 65; *Corporaciones* 64; Council for the National Economy 64; *dictablanda* 62; *El Democrata* 63; Nazi sympathisers 65; Partido Nacional (PN) 63; Partido Ruralista (PR) 65; social Catholicism 63; Soviet Union 65; Spanish Republic 65; Unión Cívica del Uruguay (UCU) 63–4
US 102; New Deal 99

Valois, Georges 11
Vargas, Getúlio 18, 20, 27–9, 64, 68–9, 71, 72, 74–6, 78, 111; "father of the poor" 79
Viana, Oliveira 70, 72, 73, 78, 110
Viera, Julio (Lieutenant-Colonel) 60
Villegas, Silvio 101

Weber, Max 12

Yrigoyen, Hipólito 27, 31, 33–4

Zenón Uribe, Rafael Víctor 103

For Product Safety Concerns and Information please contact our EU
representative GPSR@taylorandfrancis.com
Taylor & Francis Verlag GmbH, Kaufingerstraße 24, 80331 München, Germany

www.ingramcontent.com/pod-product-compliance
Lightning Source LLC
Chambersburg PA
CBHW060347250426
43669CB00056B/2511